THE ROUGH GUIDE TO

POKER

by
Iain Fletcher

Additional contributions by
Jamie Walters

Credits

The Rough Guide To Poker
Editor: Andrew Heritage
Layout: bounford.com
Picture Research: Maria Gibbs
Proofreading: Ailsa C. Heritage
US Consultant: Chuck Wills
Production: Julia Bovis and Katherine Owers

**This edition was prepared by Heritage Editorial
and bounford.com for Rough Guides Ltd.**

Publishing Information

This first edition published October 2005 by
Rough Guides Ltd, 80 Strand, London WC2R 0RL
345 Hudson St, 4th Floor, New York 10014, USA
Email: mail@roughguides.com

Distributed by the Penguin Group:
Penguin Books Ltd, 80 Strand, London WC2R 0RL
Penguin Putnam, Inc., 375 Hudson Street, NY 10014, USA
Penguin Group (Australia), 250 Camberwell Road, Camberwell, Victoria 3124, Australia
Penguin Books Canada Ltd, 10 Alcorn Avenue, Toronto, Ontario, Canada M4V 1E4
Penguin Group (New Zealand), Cnr Rosedale and Airborne Roads, Albany, Auckland, New
Zealand

Printed in Italy by LegoPrint S.p.A.

Typeset in Rotis

256 pages; includes index

A catalogue record for this book is available from the British Library

ISBN 10: 1-84353-669-2

ISBN 13: 978-1-84353-669-7

1 3 5 7 9 8 6 4 2

10

Contents

INTRODUCTION

If it was only the occasional hour that I spent online, staring at pathetic hole cards, wondering why every other player seems to get pocket aces, I would never have considered writing this guide to poker. (Don't worry about the lingo – you'll soon pick it up. And in the meantime, there's a handy glossary on p.37.) But it isn't. It's days, weeks even, and still I love the game. Every player is a unique opponent, every hand presents a different challenge, and every win still brings a triumphant rush.

The losses alone end up eating away at my time, as I catch myself going through the inevitable post-mortem of my play and my betting strategy. Was I too aggressive? Too timid? Did I act out of position or did I just get out-drawn on the river? Whatever the reason, ultimately it's just another hard luck story to mentally file away and never admit to in public.

But I'm not alone. There are millions – *tens* of millions – like me in the world, logging on to computers, cranking up the Internet and using it for what Tim Berners-Lee never remotely intended – gambling at cards.

Texas Hold'em is my favourite game, popularized as it has been by TV exposure. In this version, the best possible starting hand is a Pair of Aces. In theory, it should win you the game. But it doesn't always. And that is the beauty of poker. You can never be sure what the next turn of a card will bring.

It is the Internet and TV that have fuelled the recent poker explosion. People are starting to learn how compelling, how utterly tantalizing, a game of cards can be. Hollywood has known this for years, of course, using card sessions to dramatise the psychological torments of their big-screen heroes (and anti-heroes). Indeed, poker has

♦ ♣ ♥ ♠

cropped up in hundreds of movies, not least *The Cincinnati Kid*, and makes for a potent metaphor. Over in Washington, meanwhile, many US presidents have been keen players, from the current incumbent, George W. Bush (not surprising considering he hails from Texas, the very heartland of poker), back to Harry Truman, who played throughout his army years, and kept up his chops when in the White House. (Indeed, he, gave Winston Churchill a good licking at the felt in 1946.)

But though poker has been played by the rich and powerful, and by the celebrities of stage and screen, nobody really cares who you are or where you are from. Your money is good and your cards count the same as everyone else's.

But why am I explaining all this when I could be playing? See you in cyberspace, or across the green felt...

Iain Fletcher
September 2005

Picture credits

A Note on Money

Monetary sums in this book have largely been expressed in dollars, because so much of the story of poker is set in the US, and most major tournaments occurred until recently in the US. Furthermore, most online sites operate and bet in $US.

THE GAME
OF POKER

POKER TODAY

Poker Comes in from the Cold

The growth of poker, both online and in the real world, is nothing short of a phenomenon. In the space of the last decade, it has developed from being niche and underground – frowned upon by many, properly understood by few, and played predominantly in the US – into the most popular card game on the planet. These days, people can't seem to get enough of it. US and European TV schedules have become stuffed with live poker tournaments. Casino poker rooms, in their death throes by the end of the 1990s, are now commonplace and regularly packed with players. Playing at home has never been so popular, with an ever-increasing number of friends wanting to take money off each other. And as for the Internet... well, finally it looks like something might just challenge pornography as the most popular and lucrative online activity.

The Internet, of course, offers a technical format and useability which makes it uniquely suited to online gambling, and it may be that poker has provided the Holy Grail which eluded online entrepreneurs for so long: how to make real money out of a virtually free technology. Internet poker has become simply massive and it is now a multi-billion dollar industry.

The scale of its success is staggering. Gibraltar-based Party Gaming, the company that in 2001 launched the world's most popular poker site, Party Poker, makes an estimated $100,000 profit an hour and is now officially a bigger company than British Airways or ICI, ranking higher than both of them on the London Stock Exchange. The Scandinavian-run Poker Room, which is third on the list of largest poker sites, has more than four million people registered from 140 countries. Seven thousand new players will register there today, and at this very moment, about 12,000 people will be engaged in a poker

♦ ♣ ♥ ♠

An indication of poker's recent elevation to respectability is the appearance of a syndicated column from the multiple WSOP winner Doyle Brunson in the UK's conservative weekly *The Sunday Telegraph*.

game of some description. It is a level of success unheard of in the history of gambling. Or, indeed, the Internet.

The business of poker, once seen as belonging in backrooms populated by shady characters, is now legitimate – audited by top accounting firms such as Price Waterhouse Coopers and, as an industry sector, it is considered to be among the safest investment bets around. Party Gaming (owners of Party Poker) was the first online gaming company to float and was massively successful, setting in train a rush to the stock market of others. It hasn't all been plain sailing; as with many new investment areas, the market rapidly over-heated, and in summer 2005 a careless comment by Party Poker's boss wiped millions off Party Poker's share price. The organization responded with a high-profile PR campaign, and in-your-face advertising. When England regained the cricketing Ashes from Australia at the Oval sports ground in September 2005, the most prominent image at the awards ceremony was Party Poker's banner billboard in the background.

THE BIG BUSINESS OF POKER

When **Party Gaming**, the company that owns the market-leading online poker room **Party Poker**, floated in late summer 2005, its four owners, who included former online porn purveyor Ruth Parasol, cashed in on an estimated £930 million between them. The company's chief executive, Richard Seagal, received £50 million worth of shares and the company itself entered the FTSE 100 with a valuation of about £4.5 billion. Party Poker has made a lot of people rich beyond their wildest dreams.

And it seems others want a piece of the stock market action. With more than 1,000 online poker sites generating $2 billion a year – that's equal to 40 per cent of the entire Las Vegas revenue last year – it's only a matter of time before others cash in on the stock exchange. A number of the Party Gaming's closest rivals are planning to do it sooner rather than later.

The Costa Rica-based **Pokerstars.com**, which currently has 10 per cent of market share, is number two to Party Poker and looks set to become the next publicly-owned poker company. In August 2005, they announced plans to move their operations to the Isle of Man off the west coast of England, a move that is seen as a precursor to a stock market flotation. The group, controlled by the Israeli Scheinberg family, has secured a license to trade on the island and has been attracted by significant tax breaks. Indeed, the Isle of Man authorities are actively seeking to entice online gambling operations to move their businesses there and have made significant changes to their duty regime, as well as announcing they will be scrapping corporation tax in April 2006. Indeed, Bill Mummery, a former director of **Betinternet**, among the first online gambling operations to transfer to the island, is now head of e-gaming development for the Isle of Man.

♦ ♣ ♥ ♠

The *Party Poker* home page reflects the high-end design and virtually-real quality of many of the best online sites. ©PartyPoker.com

How attractive the island will be to online gaming operations is unclear – Gibraltar is still a popular spot, being home to both **Party Gaming** and **Cassava Enterprises** (who run **888.com** and **Pacific Poker**). But in terms of flotation, the attraction seems to be irresistible, and there is a long list of online gambling operations – including the **Gala Group**, **Coral Eurobet**, **Cassava Enterprises**, **Trident Gaming**, **Betfair** and **Poker Room** – looking to move there.

But will poker shares be a good bet for investors? Some are sceptical. Although times are good now, some investors say it can't continue indefinitely, and the continued attempts by the US government to ban online gambling through legislation are a big potential problem.

Annual tournaments such as the *World Series Of Poker* (WSOP) have become hugely
popular spectator events – the *World Poker Tour* (WPT) was developed specifically for TV.

The poker industry has reached these prodigious heights in less
than a decade. The first online poker room, Planet Poker, was not
launched until 1998 with the next big player, Paradise Poker (still
one of the leading online poker rooms), hitting the scene in 1999.
Other leading sites such as Pokerstars did not launch until 2001. And
although they enjoyed initial success, it took a different medium to
turn them into the phenomenon they have become. All the clever
software and smart marketing in the world could not have done as
much for online poker as TV has.

Poker on the Box

It is televised poker that has been rightly credited with lighting
the fuse that set off the global poker explosion. That part of the
story began in 1998 with the British show Late Night Poker. While

attempts to put poker on TV had been tried before – US sports network ESPN have been broadcasting recorded bits of the World Series of Poker (WSOP) since 1993 – none had been a hit with viewers. Watching Texas Hold'em – in which each player has two cards that, in the majority of hands, remain unexposed – was just dull. Either nobody had worked out that viewers needed to see the hole cards, or nobody had worked out a way of exposing them just to the TV cameras while keeping them hidden from the live players at the table. The solution, when it came, was blindingly simple: put cameras under the table that could capture the hole cards through small glass windows. Late Night Poker was the first programme to put the idea to use and it revolutionized the viewing experience. Suddenly every aspect of a game could be included in the coverage. Viewers could see when players were bluffing, trapping or playing a hand they really shouldn't. A player's tactics could be comprehensively analysed. Pundits, so important to TV, could find something to talk about. With the correct commentary – brilliantly done on Late Night Poker with the inimitable and ever-excitable Jesse May – the game suddenly became an absorbing and sometimes thrilling spectator experience. It was an unqualified hit, regularly attracting more than a million viewers despite being aired after midnight.

Other UK shows, like the Ladbrokes Poker Million, soon jumped on the bandwagon, but it was when the American cable networks picked up on the idea that the poker boom well and truly started. The World Poker Tour, a series of tournaments designed exclusively for TV, was aired on the Travel Channel in the US for the first time in 2003 and was an immediate ratings success, quickly becoming the most watched show in the channel's history. Millions regularly tuned in to see a mixture of pro-am celebrity tournaments – involving the

THE RULE OF LAW

One very dark cloud on online poker's horizon is the issue of its legality. While it is legal and regulated in the UK and various countries around the Caribbean, its status within the US – whose citizens make up 70 per cent of the online poker-playing public - has never been clear, and remains ambiguous to this day. Some US states have specific laws against online gambling of any kind, and no states offer online gaming licenses. Considering that owning an online gaming site without proper licensing is illegal, this makes running one inside the US very dangerous indeed.

However, the nature of the Internet and the fact that sites are run from such locations as Gibraltar and Costa Rica will make banning, or even just regulating, online poker a very difficult proposition. But that's not stopping the US government from trying. Online gambling has been described as 'uniquely evil' by one US senator, and American legislators have made repeated and ever-more creative attempts to curb the nation's seemingly insatiable desire for online gambling.

The latest initiative is to prohibit people from being able to deposit money with online gambling operations. A proposed bill would block banks and credit card companies from allowing their customers to use their accounts for online bets, a move that, if successful, would massively reduce the customer base and revenue for all online gambling companies.

But there is a strong business lobby in the US that says their government's blind spot towards the lucrative online gambling market is costing the US Treasury millions in potential tax revenue – money that is being gleefully accepted in other countries of the world. With a number of online gambling firms expressing an interest in relocating to the US if it were guaranteed they would not be prosecuted, this lobby's view is hard to ignore.

♦ ♣ ♥ ♠

likes of Don Cheadle, Meatloaf and Mickey Rooney – and high-stake professional competitions, with buy-ins as high as US$25,000 and prize pools greater than US$2.5 million.

ESPN soon saw the potential and, in 2003, introduced under-the-table cameras to their coverage. They saw their ratings rocket. And so followed a slew of tournaments on a variety of channels, including Celebrity Poker on Bravo and the Heads-Up Poker Challenge on NBC. Indeed, when national network NBC broadcast the World Poker Tour Battle of Champions as an alternative to pre-Superbowl entertainment in 2004, it drew in millions of viewers. Never before had so many been drawn away from the Superbowl programming, and at this point it was clear to all that poker had hit the US mainstream. The once backroom game was now firmly established as a part of popular culture. And nobody benefited more than the poker websites, with the industry in general growing from estimated revenues of $92 million in 2002, to $365 million in 2003, and to more than $1 billion in 2004.

The Revival of the Gaming Rooms

As demand to play grew online, so it did offline, a fact that gave casinos in the US (and indeed the world over) something of a problem. For years, poker rooms in Las Vegas had been virtually unused – new casinos were being built without them and many older ones went as far as to remove them entirely, citing a lack of demand as the cause. This may well be true, but it is more likely that casinos have actively discouraged poker over the years, seeing it as a low revenue game. The odds aren't nearly as attractive to the house as they are in games such as blackjack and roulette – games that are weighted heavily in favour of the casino, and which will always win a massive chunk of the total money bet. In poker, however, the vast majority of the money bet will end up with the players. Poker is not played against the house, but against other poker players, and so the only way casinos can profit is by charging entry fees for tournaments or taking a regular 'rake' – basically a rent charge for playing at the table. Further, poker tables take up a lot of room, making nothing like as much profit per square metre as a slot machine does (this has been variously reckoned as $300-$400 per hour; the profit ratio is estimated to be 10 to 1 in slot machines' favour). Vegas' most unintelligent and unchallenging way to gamble is, for some strange reason, by far its most popular ... and, of course, you can pack a lot of slot machines into a poker table's footprint.

But the boom came, and suddenly huge numbers of people who had seen poker on television and played it online wanted to play it in casinos. There was a huge resurgence of interest from punters wanting to taste a traditional poker room and experience the face-to-face buzz of a real-life game. The casinos had no choice but to respond, and as a result poker rooms have been opening, reopening and filling up all over the US and Europe. In truth, it's still not a huge revenue-generator for them. But casinos have started to see its value. A Nevada Gaming Control Board research analyst has estimated that revenue from poker in Las Vegas reached almost $6 million in 2003, and there is little doubt it has climbed since then. And on top of the direct cash benefit, the indirect benefit of drawing more and more people into the casinos is undeniable. Like a big boxing match or a Siegfried and Roy show, poker may not make that much money by itself, but it gets the punters through the door and spending elsewhere. The casinos have realized this, and have now embraced the poker revolution to such an extent that most now offer poker lessons.

Can you imagine them doing the same for roulette? Of course not. If they did, their cash flow would dry up – the only sensible advice with a game such as that is don't play, it's all based on luck. Poker, on the other hand, as any good player will tell you, is a game of skill. Sure, it is classified as gambling and anyone who tells you luck is not involved is lying; if you have played more than once you are virtually guaranteed to have had a bad beat and lost a pot you had every right to win. But on the whole the game is about expertise and talent, making it the only one in the casino that is. What's more, the house won't kick you out if you win too much – they don't care who takes the money, as they get their cut regardless. It's this combination of factors that make it possible for those who have mastered the game to become professionals. There is a living to be made from touring the world playing in poker tournaments, and for some it is very lucrative.

Living the Life
There is also big money to be made online. It's not just those running the websites who are making fortunes from Internet poker – good players also win big in cyberspace from the regular tournaments, many of which have prize pools in excess of $1 million. But the nature of the game is slightly different online. Body language and poker faces are taken out of the equation, with players having to rely on betting patterns and reaction times to see through bluffs. The game is also played considerably faster on the Internet: a casino table will get through about 30 hands an hour; an online table averages as many as 80. Despite these differences, the mathematical principles of the game remain the same. Good hands are just as good online as they are in the casino, and the money won is every bit as real. It's true that some top players, especially the

POKER IN YOUR POCKET

One more major concern for the future of poker on the Internet is the challenge that will come from mobile phone technology. Texas Hold'em games that can be downloaded to handsets are already on the market and proving popular. They are currently, on the whole, no-money games that are played for fun. But software developers – notably **MobileGamingNow** – have started releasing versions that allow cash games between multiple simultaneous users. These enable you to play other people for money, just as you would on the Internet, from your handset.

Although the technology is in its infancy, some commentators are predicting an explosion in mobile poker that will mirror and even outstrip what we have seen online. A new report by Juniper Research estimates that, by 2009, mobile gambling services will generate revenues of more than $19.3 billion, nearly a third of all mobile-entertainment revenues. Java-enabled graphics, colour-filled screens and 3G networking combine to provide a service that rivals traditional

old guard, sneer at the virtual version, but most have accepted and adopted it, some going as far as to endorse the poker rooms they play in. Top pros Phil Hellmuth and David 'Devilfish' Uliot support UltimateBet, Mike Sexton and Shana Hiatt are spokespeople for Party Poker, and multi-WSOP title-winner Doyle Brunson even has his own site called Doyle's Room.

The crossover is not just one way, however. Just as people from the world of live poker have infiltrated cyberspace, so the reverse has happened. Indeed, two of the last three winners of the headline Texas Hold'em event at the WSOP were online qualifiers. In 2003, 27-year-old Chris Moneymaker won the title and the $2.5 million prize after winning a $40 buy-in tournament on Pokerstars.com.

gambling methods. Although the number of mobile phone handsets which support the new software is limited, it is expected that future software versions will be released with improved compatibility.

Despite optimistic predictions based on the rapid success of other mobile phone technologies – facilities such as digital photography, video and music downloading – opinion is divided upon whether mobile phone gambling is a potential high-earner or destined to remain a niche market.

Some believe the often high cost of mobile phone airtime and the limited amount of free minutes available to users on many tariffs will put off many potential players – especially as most will be used to playing online where access is relatively cheap and unmetered. The opposing side of the argument suggests the high distribution of mobile phones, and the fact that they can be used anywhere, will more than offset any such negative factors. However, the jury is still out on this, and only time will tell.

Greg 'Fossilman' Raymer, who also qualified through Pokerstars.com, followed in 2004 winning an even bigger pot of $5 million. Joseph Hachem, the 2005 champion from Australia who scooped $7.5 million, entered the traditional way, paying the $10,000 buy-in. Back on television, celebrity-amateur games such as Sky's Poker Millions have seen Soccer AM presenter Helen 'Hells Bells' Chamberlain winning £223,000 (having apparently never played a live television game before), as runner-up to warehouseman Anthony Jones.

It may not have seen a title winner but the 2005 WSOP, as it has in all recent years, saw a huge amount of prize money going to online qualifiers which proves that if you can cut it in the virtual world, you can do it in the real one too. That doesn't mean it's easy money.

While there is a lot to be won, there are also a lot of people trying to win it. Some of them don't know what they're doing but many do and, if you are one of the former, you'll be out of pocket in no time – much to the benefit of the latter. To ensure you are not fleeced, learn how to play the game properly before committing your cash to it. Both casinos and poker websites offer tutorials, and the websites offer 'play-money' games in which beginners can develop their skills without having to risk any of their cash – you would be wise to take advantage of as many of these as possible. But nothing will start you off better than reading this book. Just remember, poker is a game that takes moments to learn and a lifetime to master.

Joseph Hachem winning the 2005 World Series of Poker title and a record-breaking $7.5 million. His day job is mortgage-brokering, and he out-played the poker professionals to become the first Australian to win the title.

POKER HISTORY:
THE MYTHS, THE MOB
AND MURDER

The Origins of Poker

Poker is played the world over today, but nobody is quite sure where it came from. The origins of the game remain ill-defined and shrouded in mystery. Poker is, after all, about the tension and excitement of playing, and it's hardly surprising few have felt the need to research its past or its beginnings. Yet, though its players have understandably been far more interested in why they won or lost a game, poker has a colourful and fascinating cultural history.

Did it start in France? Or was it Persian, perhaps? The truth is, no-one really knows the real beginnings of poker. Even authoritative reference works talk only vaguely about a similar game played in the Middle East, and there is certainly evidence of a game of chance and betting, based on a deck of cards not unlike those we use today, being played there around a thousand years ago. Decks of cards feature in illustrations of everyday life from the Middle Ages, and it is clear that suited cards were in use throughout medieval Europe. Indeed, the traditional graphic illustrations of the royal cards, Jack, Queen and King, have their roots in the chivalric courtly iconography of the time. But whether these precedents have anything to do with poker is a different matter.

Early card games also feature in the writings of medieval writers like Chaucer and had become, by the 16th century, a popular feature of genre writing and painting. The dramatic work of Christopher Marlowe and Ben Jonson, and the paintings of the Italian low-life master Caravaggio and many Dutch and Flemish painters of the period, feature card games, often using the displayed cards as significant narrative symbols (he's a winner...he's a loser... he's a chancer...). Both Marlowe and Caravaggio were interested in cardplay, and both may well have died as a result of disputes at the table.

One theory is that poker is derived from a 16th-century Persian game called As Nas. This game involved 25 cards with five different suits and had many of the hands used today, such as Three of a Kind; but similar games evolved, possibly independently, in different parts of Europe, variously known as *poque* in France, and *pochespiel* or *pochen* in Germany and Eastern Europe. Meanwhile, other vying games like brag were definitely being played in Western Christendom, and these too probably were some of the roots of the modern game.

Games of chance and betting based on modern decks of cards date back at least two centuries. Among these are gin rummy, and versions of *vingt-et-un*, and blackjack. In fact, the notion of betting, for or against a winning hand, has a long heritage, and all of these, like poker, depend on a mixture of luck in the play of the cards, nerve (or lack of it) in betting, mixed with a strong element of bluff: all essential ingredients of poker play.

The Evolution of Modern Poker

What is known for sure is that poker was written about in the 1820s in America (the Oxford English Dictionary cites 1824 as the first use of the word 'poker') and then it was called the 'cheating game', but it is likely that in one form or another it had been played for several decades before this.

It became really popular, however, in the French settlement of New Orleans in the early 1800s and then later on the Mississippi steamboats and all points west. It suited the speculative natures of the gamblers, prospectors, traders and frontiersmen that dominated the West in those years. From saloons to backroom ignominy to the current staple of TV networks all over the world, poker has travelled

STEAMBOATS AND SWINDLERS

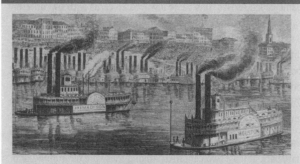

In early 19th-century America, the main transport routes in the interior, before the development of the railroads, were the waterways of the Mississippi, Missouri and Ohio rivers and their tributaries. These linked the former French settlements around New Orleans with the rapidly-growing Midwest centres of Chicago and St. Louis to the north, the cities to the East, and the open frontier of the West. The evolution of flat-bottomed steam-driven paddle-ships literally reached new heights along these waterways, resulting in multi-decked floating palaces. Passengers with time on their hands made for easy pickings for professional cardsharps. As early as 1835 the city of Vicksburg had banned them. Nevertheless, by 1860, some 20,000 professional gamblers were working the 10,000 or so steamers plying the rivers.

Cheating was rife, not just dependent on sleight of hand, but also involving marking and trimming cards, and sleeve, breastplate and vest 'holdouts' which secretly stored crucial winning cards. The Kepplinger holdout was an ingenious contraption of springs and wires worn under the clothes, and operated by knee movements, which could shoot a winning card into the gambler's hand through his sleeve.

♦ ♣ ♥ ♠

a long way since the Persians started playing with suited cards 400 years ago. If they did, that is.

Some varieties of poker in their modern forms appear to have emerged in the early years of the 19th century in America. This is hardly surprising, given the rich admixture of cultures which formed the 'melting-pot' of races, nationalities, creeds and cultures which flooded across the Atlantic to the New World in the century or so after 1820. From the gambling 'hells' of the Lower East Side of Manhattan, where most European immigrants made landfall right up to the years following World War II, to the westward progress of the 'frontier', for most of the immigrant peoples gambling was an integral part of life: many had, after all, gambled everything on a new life on a new continent.

To the south, New Orleans was the one of the main destinations for French and southern European immigrants. All of these newcomers brought with them their languages and cultures, and their games and recreations. Poker in its various forms emerged from an admixture of a wide variety of different vying and card games.

Only in it for the Gold
It was not just the immigrant 'greenhorns' who drew the attention of the cardsharps. With the discovery of gold in California, Colorado and the Yukon, a whole new wave of aspiring millionaires arrived on the West Coast, seeking their fortunes. When endless days of digging and sieving failed to pan out, the attraction of winning a fast buck at the table became irresistible. The saloons of the far West became notorious for the voracity of their proprietors. In the 1850s several cardsharps were lynched by vigilantes in California.

WILD BILL HICKOK

Wild Bill is such a well-known character from the West that it is difficult to separate fact from fiction. It is said that US President George W Bush is descended from Hickok's mother, and that Hickok himself was marshal, gambler, sheriff, gunslinger, saloon owner, entertainer, prospector and just about everything in between. A colourful character, and great self-publicist, his career was by no means unique, but provides one of the mother lodes of the American myth of the West. He was inducted, very posthumously, into the Poker Hall of Fame in 1979.

What is known for sure is that he died on August 2, 1876, shot in the back while playing in Saloon Number Ten, in Deadwood, Dakota Territory. His murderer, Jack McCall, shot him in revenge for the death of his brother, and the hand he was holding was two Pair, Aces and Eights which ever since have been known as the 'Dead Man's Hand'. What is not known is the kicker – the fifth card he was holding.

James Butler Hickok was born in Illinois on May 27, 1837. Like many young men of that time, he left home to work on the trails and in the new frontier towns. He was at various times a wagon-master, scout for the Union army during the Civil War, and served with Custer's 7th Cavalry during the Indian Wars. It was from a dispute at a card table with fellow gambler, David Tutt, that he earned his reputation as a gunslinger. They duelled in the public square of Springfield, Missouri at 6 pm on 21 July,1865, Hickok shooting Tutt through the heart.

Dandy and extrovert, Hickok's flowing mane of hair and taste for fashionable threads assured him a leading role in the myth of the West. Part of Hickok's legend was due to his affinity with the media. He developed his own publicity, bragging in various newspaper and magazine interviews to have killed hundreds of men but, like his

♦ ♣ ♥ ♠

sometime partner, John Wesley Hardin, he defended this by saying 'I never killed one man without good cause'.

In 1866, Hickok became Deputy US Marshal, and in 1869 was elected Sheriff of Ellis County, Kansas but, after shooting two troublemakers, the citizens sacked him. He briefly moved to Abilene as Marshal but mostly played poker. He did shoot another two men though, the gambler Phil Coe and, accidentally, a policeman friend, Mike Williams. When he moved on it was to tour with Buffalo Bill Cody and his Wild West Show in 1872-73. In 1876 he married a widow, Mrs Agnes Lake, some 11 years his senior.

'I never killed one man without good cause'.

Someone who got away lightly was described by Cody in 1876. Watching a game, he thought that Hickok was dozing off, and not noticing that another player was dropping useful cards into his hat, on his lap. The tension mounted, the pot being consistently raised, when the man with the hat suddenly raised with $200. Hickok, unperturbed, matched the raise and, as his opponent covered it, pushed a pistol into his face, saying: 'I'm calling the hand that's in your hat'. He was not always altogether honourable; on another occasion, when in danger of being sharped, he called a raise with the last of his dollars. At the showdown, he lost but, drawing his irons, he said, 'I also have a Pair of Sixes, and they beat everything'.

As to that kicker, the transcript of McCall's trial has a witness claiming (appropriately) that it was the Jack of Diamonds. Deadwood Museum supposedly have the actual card from the hand, a Five of Diamonds. The important thing though is that Dead Man's Hand is not a particularly good hand and, if you want to do it properly, the Aces and Eights should both be black suits.

As the Frontier lands filled, so other opportunities developed. Among these were the 'cow towns' – places at which the cattle drovers met the railheads, linking them to the slaughterhouses of Chicago and the East. Boomtowns like Abilene, Denver, Dodge City, and Tombstone sprang up, and it was here where the Eastern immigrants met the Mexicans, mountain-men, rousters, rustlers and cowhands. And here too, so many legends of the West – gunfighters, lawmen, bank robbers, train men, prospectors, desperadoes, pistoleros, comancheros and the like – took root. And it was fertile ground. In truth, there weren't many real legends: most were scumbags,

chancers and wastrels, but the East Coast newspapers, dime-novel publishers, and pioneer showbiz ventures like Buffalo Bill's Wild West Show, which travelled across America and Europe in the last quarter of the century, helped to build the legend. So did journalists like Henry Morgan Stanley (who later famously tracked down Dr Livingstone in Africa) and Ned Buntline, who latched on to colourful characters and built the myth of the West.

The gambling games which rode the westward advance of the Frontier found enthusiastic followers among the Mexicans and Native American inhabitants, and even today ready games can be found on many Indian reservations.

An essential part of that myth was gambling. Ability at gunplay, drinking, and behaviour at the table and in bed were central aspects of the Western legend. As was honour: despite a conspicuous inability to keep guns, livers and libidos under control, characters like Wild Bill Hickock, John Wesley Hardin, Doc Holliday and the Earp brothers have been passed down to us as, at best, heroes and, at worst, fallen angels.

The reality was somewhat different. Although professional gamblers did exist in the 'Wild West' of late 19th-century America, for most of them gambling was a side-bet. Running a brothel or a saloon was a better guarantee of an income, and one that was less likely to get you on the wrong side of the law or a Colt '45. Hickok, the Earps, Holliday and Hardin all ran saloons and worked as hired guns, Hardin also running a timber business. His inventive self-promotion extended to providing customers with a unique business card – an Ace card individually 'aireated' with bullet holes to order.

Nevertheless, gambling, and especially poker, which could be played with a simple pack of cards, unlike in fact more popular and easily-suckered games like faro (which required a fixed table), wheel of fortune (which required a wheel), or stuss (which merely required 'greenhorns' fresh from the immigrant boats) was a vital source of income for many entrepreneurs.

Deadlier Than The Male

Although we are now familiar and comfortable with women competing in most areas of sport, poker stars in skirts long predate the era of female emancipation and 'Women's Lib'. While current poker stars like Mimi Rogers and Annie Duke cannot be called the direct descendants of some of the female rounders of

THE ROUNDER'S ARSENAL

Easily-concealed weapons were an essential part of the professional gambler's kit. They ranged from boot- and sleeve-daggers to knuckledusters, and interesting combinations of both, often elaborately decorated. Regular handguns were frequently sawn off to create 'belly' guns, and soon Colt, Smith & Wesson and Starr were producing tailor-made versions, often coyly marketed through catalogues as 'ladies guns'. But it was Henry Deringer who originally came up with a miniature single-shot .45. His imitators produced a wide variety of similar firearms, and used (and misspelt) his name as Derringer. Often with two or four chambers, attachable to fob chains or concealed in the palm, these weapons were wildly inaccurate and practically ineffectual beyond about six feet, but were presumably enough to deter anyone at the table from daring to cheat. Except the man with the gun.

the 19th century, nor can they be regarded as the first queens of the green baize. Both sharpshooter Annie Oakley and sometime robber roustabout Belle Starr excelled at the table. The career of Belle Siddons ranged across the American continent from spying during the Civil War, taking up gambling when widowed in 1869, running casinos in Wichita, Denver and Deadwood under the names Madame Vestal and Lurline Monte Verde, and becoming the mistress of stagecoach robber Archie McLaughlin. She wound up an opium addict in San Francisco. Another was English-born Alice Iver, or 'Poker Alice', who when widowed young took up full-time gambling, smoked, carried guns, killed a man, and retired after being tried for running a gambling den and brothel.

♦ ♣ ♥ ♠

Prohibition and the Mob

In the years following the Civil War, most states cracked down on gambling, particularly 'bank' games in which the punter bets against the house. There was also a racist slant on the West Coast where Chinese gambling dens were targeted. The anti-gambling lobby was part of a movement that tried to 'legislate morality', which ultimately also led to the prohibition of alcohol, although there was a progressive element to it, in that professional cardsharps fleeced the poor as well as the well-to-do. But in reality, there was little enforcement of gambling legislation, certainly in the West.

Organized crime in America had long had an interest in gambling, running its own rackets such as the numbers game and enforced lotteries, whilst providing secure locations for every game that could be rigged from blackjack to roulette, and taking a 'skim' on any game they couldn't raise a vig on.

During the Prohibition years, the Mob was pretty much funded by illicit alcohol, prostitution and gambling scams, but with the repeal of the alcohol ban, their main revenue stream, ironically, dried up. Charles 'Lucky' Luciano, who gained control of the New York 'families' in 1931, saw the obvious potential of the narcotics trade as a vital new source of income. However, the FBI's increasingly devious means of inhibiting organized criminal activity, evidenced by their successful prosecution of the Chicago 'Outfit' boss, Al Capone, on a humble tax evasion rap, meant that crime on the multi-national, industrial scale that Luciano envisaged, needed to clean up its act, and crucially, its money.

It was the Russian emigré Meyer Lansky, Luciano's collaborator in murderously reorganizing the New York families into 'The Syndicate' in the early '30s, who recognized the potential of large-scale casinos

LAS VEGAS

New York mobster Meyer Lansky connived with an associate, the slick West Coast bookmaking operator and sometime killer, Benjamin 'Bugsy' Siegel, to exploit the relaxation of gaming laws in Nevada. Reno was the first Nevada city to open up gambling as a significant money-earner, but further south (and again only a few miles from the California state line, and only 200 miles from Los Angeles) the crossroads watering town of Las Vegas ('The Meadows') offered a great opportunity. An opportunity made even greater by the construction of the Hoover Dam. The purpose-built workers' dormitory town, Boulder City, eschewed gambling. Originally little more than a one-horse town of a few shacks and a handful of gaming joints, by 1932, a year after Nevada relaxed its gaming laws, Las Vegas welcomed and entertained over 100,000 tourists. Within a decade, legitimate ventures such as El Rancho Vegas and the Last Frontier were becoming established. In 1943, Siegel set about spending Mob money to create a brand-new phenomenon: the one-stop luxury gambling resort in the form of The Flamingo hotel and casino, offering, in addition to gaming rooms, top-class rooms and suites, restaurants, cocktail bars, a swimming pool, golf course, watered lawns and all mod-cons, including air conditioning. The Mob advanced him $2 million, but the final budget excdeeded $6 million, which included construction company skims which Siegel and his girlfriend deposited in Switzerland. Siegel laid the groundplan for what Las Vegas has become, although even he could not have envisaged the hideous baroque grandeur of Caesar's Palace or The Mirage.

Siegel paid the price for his avarice in 1947 when a hit man's bullet went through his head, and the Mob are now for the most part long gone, but part of the glamour of the place is its tainted past. A giant washing-machine for Mob funds, it nevertheless indelibly

♦ ♣ ♥ ♠

stained some of its more high-profile associates; peerless crooner Frank Sinatra, whose regular performances with the Rat Pack at the Sands casino, designed to publicize the place and pull in the punters, earned him a flat fee plus points in every Mob-run casino. In return, Sinatra and his chums managed to make gambling socially legitimate and glamorous, drawing both gaming and drinking out of the shadows of Prohibition, to form a central icon of the Eisenhower and Kennedy high-rolling culture. America on a Straight, with the Camelot Clan as the Royal Flush.

The Rat Pack posing outside their favourite Vegas playground, the Sands. From the left JFK's brother-in-law Peter Lawford, Frank 'The Voice' Sinatra, Sammy Davis Jr., the joker in the pack, and Dean Martin.

♦ ♣ ♥ ♠

as powerful money-laundering machines. The punters go in, buy their chips with clean money, and redeem their chips at the end of the session, entirely innocently, receiving dirty money. Initially, Lansky targeted the offshore funspot of Cuba's Havana but, with Nevada's legalization of gambling in 1931, new possibilities opened up closer to home. And Vegas as we know it was born.

In the early, heady days, Las Vegas was a success partly because of its proximity to the 'City of the Angels' and other playgrounds like Palm Springs, and partly its closeness to the burgeoning Cold War military installations in the desert lands of the Southwest. The keys to its success were the democracy of the automobile, and the

The Pioneer was one of the first outstanding neon landmarks on the Strip. It has since been revamped as the New Pioneer.

POKER IN THE WHITE HOUSE

Poker, it seems, is no stranger to the Oval Office. While untold hands have certainly been played at the highest rank, it is President Harry S. Truman who holds the trump for coining the phrase "the buck stops here" in a political context. Appropriate maybe for a seemingly modest but decisive man, who called the bet on deploying the A-bomb against Japan and, at a stroke, created the Cold War and M.A.D. stalemate for half a century. Amarillo Slim boasts of playing the cheating game with both Lyndon B. Johnson and Richard Nixon. The former bluffed everyone over whether he was bombing Laos or not, while Tricky Dicky decisively lost his showdown with the Senate committee on Watergate. It was that sweaty upper lip which also lost him the televised pre-vote debate with Kennedy in 1962.

growth of the airline industry. 'Old Blue Eyes' might have invited his listeners to 'Come Fly With Me', but he was mainly commuting between his compound in Palm Springs, his holiday home in Lake Tahoe, and Rat Pack 'Summits' in Vegas, Atlantic City and South Beach, Miami in his private jet. This was a lifestyle that everyone wanted a taste of, and the package tour to Las Vegas fast became the domestic holiday which everyone in the States aspired to. Ironically, the aeronautical giant Boeing even planned to transfer its headquarters from Seattle to Vegas, but reconsidered due to the city's Mob associations. The craven impotence of the city administration was soon highlighted by the rapid, unstructured sprawl of development. In the shadow of Siegel's extravagant Flamingo, numerous other casino/hotels sprouted out of the desert.

Las Vegas is the only million-plus city in the world which is less than 75 years old. In addition to the top-rank attraction of gaming in all its forms (probably more than you can imagine), it is still the showbiz city. A residency at any of the larger houses is the tired entertainer's dream-ticket; in the wake of Sinatra and his cronies, witness the career-saving contracts offered to Englebert Humperdinck, Tom Jones, Celine Dion, Elton John et al. We may today be astonished by the commercial success of television gaming and online poker ventures in the last decade, but this is merely the tip of an iceberg that calved four generations ago, in a desert.

Death in Vegas

Las Vegas may declare itself free of its Mob associations, and now promotes itself as an ideal 'family' resort, but the recent murky death of a member of one of the city's founding families rocked the city like an earthquake. It was a scandal that gripped the gambling capital of the world. On September 17, 1998 Ted Binion, son of the legendary Benny Binion, the founder of Binion's Horseshoe casino in downtown Las Vegas, was found dead in his home.

Marks on his body suggested murder and, in May 2000, his girlfriend, Sandy Murphy, and 'business associate' Rick Tabish were arrested, tried, and convicted of his murder. Both received life sentences. However, aptly for a town where nothing is what it seems, their convictions were overturned in 2003, Tabish remaining in jail while Murphy was released and a retrial ordered by the Nevada Supreme Court. That started in November 2004 and, when it was completed in early 2005, both were acquitted of murder but found guilty on three counts each of conspiracy to commit grand larceny and burglary. The sentences handed down were between one and five years, but Murphy proved immediately eligible for

BINION'S HORSESHOE: THE STORY OF A CASINO

One of the most colourful characters to emerge on the Vegas scene in its early years was Texan-born Benny Binion, gambler, promoter and founder of the Horseshoe casino.

1949 Binion mounts a five-month poker game between Johnny Moss and Nick 'the Greek' Dandolos.

1951 Binion builds Horseshoe casino in downtown Las Vegas. Binion sells a share to pay legal costs back in Texas.

1964 Binion regains full control of Binion's Horseshoe but because he has no gaming license he cannot officially run the business. He is retained as a 'consultant' while his wife Jane and children (sons Jack and Ted, and daughters Becky, Barbara and Brenda) own the casino, on paper.

1970 Holds the first World Series of Poker event at the Horsehoe.

1983 Barbara Binion dies of drug overdose.

1986 Ted Binion arrested for a drug misdemeanour.

1993 & 1997 Ted Binion loses his gaming licence for drugs and mob affiliations.

1998 Becky Behnen – Benny's daughter – becomes President of the Horseshoe casino and hotel after a long and protracted legal battle with her family. Jack Binion retains a small ownership. Ted Binion found dead.

1998–2004 Binion's Horseshoe faces financial ruin and investigation by the Las Vegas Gaming Board and the IRS. It closes on a number of occasions pending investigation.

2004 Harrah's Entertainment purchase Binion's Horseshoe and it is reopened for business.

2005 MTR Gaming take over full ownership of the venue and rename it Binion's Gambling Hall and Hotel. The last year that any event in the founder's WSOP tournament is held on its original site.

parole, while Tabish was still serving a previous term for extorting a business associate.

So how did Binion, the heir to a gambling empire die, and why were Tabish and Murphy accused? The reality could have walked off the pages of an Elmore Leonard novel. The story is a typical one of weakness, greed and opportunism. Binion was a colourful character – Vegas loves them – Murphy an exotic dancer and Tabish a chancer with a record of extortion, assault and drugs. Having lost thousands of dollars at the tables, Murphy started dancing at the Cheetah Club, a topless bar, but soon started a relationship with the flamboyant Binion. Tabish first met Ted Binion standing at a urinal.

With Binion becoming increasingly paranoid as his sister Becky started legal proceedings to gain control of the Horseshoe, he employed Tabish to remove a hoard of silver coins collected by his parents from the casino vault, and to transport them to his ranch at Pahrump. He then asked him to build a vault for their safe-keeping. The cache of coins was worth millions of dollars and it was at this vault, two days after Binion's death, that Tabish was arrested with two other men. They were using a bulldozer to break into the vault. Tabish himself admitted it was foolish but, as the jury in the retrial decided, this alone was not proof of murder.

Ted Binion had a long-standing drug problem, heroin mostly, and had enjoyed previous run-ins with the cops and the Nevada Gaming Commission. On the night he died he had injected heroin and ingested xanax, and several medical experts testified that the amounts taken could easily have caused death by overdose. But what Binion never knew was that Murphy and Tabish – his girlfriend and the man who knew the location of his secret vault – were secret

♦ ♣ ♥ ♠

lovers. In a city where money counts above all else, it looks as if they had seen an opportunity and tried to take it.

Winning From a Low Hand

Stories like that of the Binion dynasty have done little to improve gambling's profile. Online activities and, more worrying for conservative lobbies everywhere, pay-as-you-go mobile phone enterprises, have created new and attractive openings for opportunists and organized crime. That is why gambling in all its forms (except possibly horse-racing – the 'Sport of Kings') has remained on the fringes of acceptable society, and invoked much legislative debate. But they also provide lucrative ventures for legitimate entrepreneurs and investors, and a much-needed field of recreation for both serious and occasional punters. Licensing, enforced club membership, and general disapproval have marked its progress in most countries, while offshore refuges (or enlightened enclaves – take your pick) have prospered. Monaco, Macao and now the Isle of Man, have registered significant exchequer increases as a result of non-prohibitive gambling laws and beneficial tax regimes. Today the battle is joined over matters of personal liberty and customer choice. While the collapse of Soviet Communism predictably witnessed a phenomenal rash of casino openings from Budapest to Kamchatka, in the 'liberal' West, issues such as the heated debate over proposals for opening a set of 'Super Casinos' in the UK have consistently run into opposition.

Of course, as elsewhere in our customer-driven society, online operations and digital technology, mainly perfectly honest and above-board, will continue to meet consumer demands and will eventually sideline resistance by simply overtaking it.

THE LANGUAGE
OF POKER

Learning the Language

If you want to enter the world of poker and be a player, then you had better learn the language. Poker has a long-established and varied vocabulary, and if you don't understand it you won't know what is going on around you. And what happens next is you lose money. Some of the phrases are obvious and others less so and, not surprisingly for a game that requires sharp wits, some are very funny – which also makes them easier to remember.

A

ACES UP any two Pair which includes a pair of Aces.

ACTION the betting in a hand. Plenty of action means lots of chips or money being bet in the pot.

ACTIVE PLAYER a player who is still involved in a hand of poker.

AGGRESSIVE a player who bets frequently or in many hands.

AK Ace-King starting hand – derived from tennis player Anna Kournikova (looks good but rarely wins). See also Big Slick

ALL BLUE a Flush which includes either Spades or Clubs.

ALLIGATOR BLOOD a description of a player who survives a long time with a short stack.

ALL-IN when players go all-in, they put all their chips in the pot. If they lose, they are out of the game.

ALL PINK a Flush which includes either Hearts or Diamonds.

AMERICAN AIRLINES a Pair of Aces as starting cards in the hole.

ANTE a compulsory bet from all players before the cards are dealt.

AQUARIUM a poker game with a lot of fish in it.

ASSASSIN a term used to describe a player in a tournament who goes on a streak of eliminating other players.

B

BACK-DOOR most commonly used to describe a playable hand that the player was not originally trying to make.

BACK RAISE the action of reraising another player's raise.

BAD BEAT a loss when the player had the better odds of winning the hand. All poker players have a wealth of bad beat stories.

BET to put chips or a wager in the pot.

BET THE POT to bet a number of chips equivalent to those already in the pot. In pot-limit games this is the maximum bet allowed.

BICYCLE see wheel

BIG BET in a limit game the big bet is the larger of the two bets. For instance in $10-$20 Hold'em the big bet is $20.

BIG BLIND a compulsory bet twice the amount of the small blind. These ensure a pot has action. See blinds

BIG LICK Six-Nine (6-9), hopefully requires no further explanation.

BIG SLICK slang for an Ace-King starting hand. See also AK

BLANK a card dealt that helps nobody.

Big Slick

BLIND GAME a game which requires blinds.

Boat

BLINDS the small blind and the big blind are compulsory bets made before any cards are dealt. The small blind is to the left of the dealer and the big blind the next player to the left of the small blind.

BLUFF a bet that a player makes but hopes will not be called, as he or she suspects that another player has the winning hand.

BOARD cards on the board are shared by all players. Also known as community cards.

BOARDCARD a community card placed in the centre of a table in Texas Hold'em or Omaha.

BOAT a Full House. For example, Three of a Kind and a Pair, so King-King-King-Seven-Seven is a boat. Also known as a full boat.

BOTTOM PAIR the lowest Pair in a hand.

BOXED CARD a card which (accidentally) appears face-up in a pack.

BRING-IN an enforced bet in Stud poker made by the player who has the lowest upcard.

BROADWAY the best possible Straight: Ten-Jack-Queen-King-Ace.

BROKEN a broken game is no longer in action.

BULLETS a Pair of Aces in the hole. Also known as American Airlines and Pocket Rockets.

BURN a card is burnt (discarded, face down) before dealing the flop, turn or river. This is done so no-one can recognize the top card of the deck from a blemish or bend.

BUTTON or dealer button: a disc that shows who is the dealer for that hand. Also a term for the dealer.

BUTTON GAME a game in which a dealer button is used.

BUY-IN the minimum sum of money required to enter a game.

C

CALIFORNIA LOWBALL Ace-to-Five lowball, using a Joker.

CALL to equal the bet or raise of an opponent, and to put that amount in the pot.

CANINE a King-Nine (K-9) starting hand. Also known as the dog.

Canine

CAP each round of betting has a cap, normally of 4, so there can be a maximum of one bet and three raises. A capped game occurs when the maximum amount of raises has been reached.

CARDS SPEAK a term for the face values of the cards in a showdown.

CASH GAME a non-tournament game where players can cash in and cash out as they please. Also known as a ring game.

CHASE to play a hand that is almost certainly likely to be beaten by one other player.

CHECK to check is to not bet. If someone then bets you have to call, raise or fold. If all players check, then play moves on to next stage.

CHECK–RAISE to check hoping a following player bets, with the intention of then raising them. A ploy with a good hand and to get more money in the pot.

CHIPS poker chips are round tokens with differing values. They represent the money used to gamble in poker. In cash games they exactly represent the money used to purchase them, but in tournaments an entry fee can bring an equal chip stack for each player (for example, a $10 online tournament could have a starting chip stack of 1000 for each player).

COLD CALL when a player calls a bet which has been raised. Usually done in late position.

COLD CARDS when players are getting no good cards to play with, they are getting cold cards.

COLLECTION a fee charged by the house for a game, either taken from each player or from the pot.

COLLECTION DROP a fee charged by the house for each hand dealt.

COLOUR CHANGE to change the chips from one denomination to another.

COLT 45 the Four and Five of Spades.

Colt 45

COMMON CARD in Stud poker, a card dealt face up to be used by all players. This occurs when there are not enough cards left in the deck to deal each player a card.

COMMUNITY CARDS in Texas Hold'em and Omaha, cards dealt face up to be shared by all players. Also known as the board.

COMPLETE THE BET in limit poker, to increase an all-in bet to a full bet.

CONNECTED two cards are said to be connected when they are consecutive, such as Five and Six. If suited, they would be connected and of the same suit.

COWBOYS a starting hand of King-King.

CRABS a Pair of Threes in the pocket.

CUT to split the deck into two, reassembling it in a different order.

CUT-CARD the bottom card in a deck.

CUTER a Joker playing as an extra Ace in games where a 53-card pack is used.

Cowboys

CUTOFF the player immediately prior to the button or dealer.

D

DANGLER a card that doesn't fit or coordinate with other cards in a hand. In Omaha, for example, players are dealt four cards before the flop. The optimum pre-flop hands comprise four cards that all work together, such as Ten-Jack-Queen-King which will hopefully be improved by the flop. However, in a hand such as Five-Ten-Jack-Queen, the dangler is the Five.

♦ ♣ ♥ ♠

DEAD CARD a card that is not playable legally.

DEAD COLLECTION BLIND a sum paid by the dealer or button, sometimes used as a means of paying for one's seat.

DEAD HAND a hand that is not playable legally.

DEAD MAN'S HAND to have a Pair of Aces and a Pair of Eights. Made famous because it was the hand Wild Bill Hickok was holding when he was murdered at a poker table.

DEAD MONEY chips being put in a pot that have no chance of winning, or a description of a no-hoper in a tournament.

DEAL the action of giving each player their cards, or providing the community cards. Often a term for each complete section of a game, from shuffling the cards to the winning of the pot.

DEALER BUTTON see button

DEAL TWICE once betting is completed, to agree that the rest of the cards to come will win half the pot, dealing a second time to win the rest of the pot.

Dead Man's Hand

Dolly Parton

DECK a full set of cards, either 52 in Hold'em, Stud or Omaha, or 52 plus a Joker in Ace-to-Five Lowball and Draw High.

DEUCE any Two card; see also ducks

DEUCE-TO-SEVEN LOWBALL see Kansas City Lowball

DIME a dime is $1000 in gambling circles.

DISCARD in Draw poker, to throw away cards from the hand to make space for replacement cards.

DOG the canine starting hand (King-Nine, K-9).

DOLLAR a $100 bet.

DOLLY PARTON a starting hand of 9-5 in Hold'em. So-called after the Dolly Parton film and song *Working Nine to Five*.

DOMINATED a term to describe a hand in which finding outs (or replacement cards) to improve it is unlikely.

DONKEY an incompetent player.

DOOR CARD in Seven-Card Stud, a door card is a player's first face-up card.

INTO THE VERNACULAR: PHRASES FROM THE TABLE

BLUE CHIP an adjective to describe something considered to be
    very reliable or of high class, for example a blue-chip company.
    Blue chips in poker are those with the highest value.

TO CALL A BLUFF now used to describe generic situations where
    liars are questioned and found out, the phrase derives from the
    poker situation where a large bet by someone holding a weak
    hand is called, or matched, and the cards turned over.

TO FOLD UNDER PRESSURE to be unable to cope with a tough
    situation, but directly linked to the act of throwing away your
    cards at a poker table when a large raise is made.

GOING ALL-IN a recent addition to the vernacular, used to describe
    people that are totally committed to something and in many
    cases are so committed that they can no longer turn back or alter
    a course of action. In poker the term describes a situation where
    a person's remaining chips are all committed to a pot.

ON AN INSIDE STRAIGHT often used to imply someone has prior
    or secret knowledge of a situation, the term evolved from an
    advantageous poker hand whereby a player holds two halves of
    a potential run, needing one card to complete, for example Four-
    Six-Seven-Eight, needing only a Five to complete the Straight.

JACKPOT any big prize, now widely used in many forms of
    gambling, and generally used to describe any windfall. Its
    origins lie in a specific form of poker where progressive antes
    begin when no player has a pair of Jacks or better.

TO PASS THE BUCK the act of transferring responsibility on to
    others. The phrase was first used in poker, and referred to the
    buckhorn-handled knife that was passed around to signify whose
    turn it was to deal. 'The buck stops here' was first used by US
    President Harry S. Truman, a keen poker-player, to describe the
    ultimate responsibility of the Oval Office.

♦ ♣ ♥ ♠

POKER FACE someone with a good 'poker face' is a good liar and can conceal his or her emotions well.

TO RAISE THE STAKES an increased commitment to or involvement in a situation. It is derived from poker, where players raise the stakes, or increase the number of chips in a pot, on a regular basis.

THE NUTS another recent crossover, used to describe things that are very good or excellent. In poker, the nuts is a hand that cannot be beaten by any other on the table.

A poker-faced W. C. Fields.

TO UP THE ANTE to increase the importance or value of something. Derived from the poker practice of increasing the ante – a forced bet all players must pay – and thereby increasing the number of chips in a pot for any given hand.

WHEN THE CHIPS ARE DOWN a time of crisis when something is really at stake. In poker, it refers to the situation when all a player's chips are committed to a pot and the outcome is now beyond their control, because they are out of the betting.

WILD CARD a term used in poker (and other card games) to describe a playing card whose value can vary as determined by its holder. In sport, it now refers to an athlete or team selected to compete in a tournament or playoff from among those who did not initially qualify. In slang it is an unpredictable or unforeseeable factor.

♦ ♣ ♥ ♠

DOUBLE UP to double a chip stack in a single hand. This is done when a player goes all-in, is called by one other player, and wins the hand.

DOWN CARD a card dealt face down to a player – also called a hole card. In Texas Hold'em, a player gets dealt two hole cards. In Stud games, all cards are dealt face down.

DOYLE BRUNSON HAND a Ten-Two starting hand with which Brunson twice won the World Series of Poker.

DRAW to try and improve your hand on a card to come.

DRAW HIGH see Draw Poker

DRAWING DEAD to be drawing a card to make a hand, but still have no chance of winning the hand and pot: for example, to be drawing a card to make a Flush when the opponent has already made his Full House.

DRAW POKER one of the principal types of poker. The players are given the opportunity to improve their hand by discarding cards and requesting replacements, such as Draw High and Lowball. See pages 86–89

DUCKS a Pair of Twos, also known as deuces.

Ducks

E

EARLY POSITION players that have to act early in a hand, like the blinds and the next player, who is known to be under the gun.

F

FACE CARDS the royal cards: King, Queen and Jack.

FAMILY POT when many players are in a pot.

FIFTH STREET more commonly known as the river, the fifth community card in Texas Hold'em.

Face cards

FISH a bad player who will, or often does, lose their money.

FISHHOOKS a pair of Jacks in the pocket.

FIVE-CARD STUD one of the principal varieties of poker. See page 91.

FIXED-LIMIT poker with fixed bets, for example $10-$20.

FLASHED CARD a card which is partially or inadvertently exposed.

FLAT CALL to flat call is to match the number of chips of the previous bet.

FLOAT THE BOAT when a player gets the card to win on the river (or Fifth Street) when their odds are almost negligible.

FLOORPERSON in a casino, an employee who allocates seats and makes ruling decisions in case of disputes.

FLOP the first three community cards in Hold'em or Omaha, dealt together face up.

FLUSH a hand of five cards all of the same suit.

FOLD to throw a hand away, also known as to muck it.

FORCED BET a mandatory bet to begin the action in the first round of betting.

FOULED HAND another term for a dead hand, not legally playable.

FOUR OF A KIND to have four cards of the same rank in a hand. For example, to have four Threes or four Aces. Also known as quads.

FOURTH STREET the fourth community card dealt after the flop in Hold'em, also known as the turn. Also the second up card in Seven-Card Stud.

FREE CARD to allow a card to be dealt for no bet when all the players have checked.

FREE-ROLL a tournament with no entry fee or charge. Widely used by Internet poker companies, a $2000 free-roll will have $2000 of prize money put up by the poker company. Also generally, the opportunity to win something at no particular cost or risk.

FULL BOAT another term for a boat or a Full House.

FULL BUY the minimum amount of chips needed to enter a game.

FULL EMPLOYMENT used to describe a bad starting hand like Seven-Two or Nine-Four, because whoever plays these a lot will always need a day job.

FULL HOUSE a hand consisting of Three of a Kind and a Pair. Also known as a boat or full boat.

Full Employment

♦ ♣ ♥ ♠

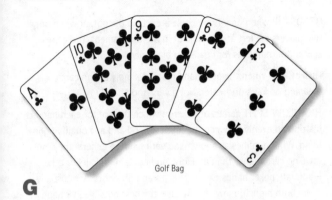

Golf Bag

G

GAY WAITER a starting hand of Queen-Three. Also known as a San Francisco Busboy.

GERMAN LESBIANS Nine-Nine, because that's what they say if you make a proposition.

GOLF BAG a Flush of Clubs.

GRINDER a small-time professional player that grinds out a living at cards. Also sometimes known as a rounder, grinders are usually found at lower-level tables winning money, but are not good enough to be successful in the big money games.

GUTSHOT an Inside Straight draw. For example, when a player needs a Five to make a Straight from Three to Seven.

H

HAND the cards that a player is using to play for the pot. Depending on the game, a hand may be all personal, or a mixture of personal and community cards.

HEADS–UP when only two people are left in the pot, or when only two players are left at the table or in the tournament. There are special tournaments for heads-up play only.

HIGH CARD when the best hand made is simply a high card, meaning no Pairs or greater. Not a very good hand.

HIGH/LOW SPLIT games of poker in which the pot for each hand is distributed evenly between the highest hand and any qualifying low hand. What qualifies as a low hand varies, but in general they must have no card higher than an Eight, and contain no Pairs or other legitimate poker hands except Flushes and Straights. Aces usually score both high and low. In this case, the best possible low hand is Ace-Two-Three-Four-Five. In some games, however, Straights, Flushes and Aces disqualify a low hand, in which case the best possible hand is Two-Three-Four-Five-Seven.

HIGH SOCIETY $10,000 in chips.

HILTON SISTERS to have a Pair of Queens, also known as Ladies or Siegfried and Roy.

HOCKEY STICKS a Pair of Sevens.

HOLD'EM see Texas Hold'em

HOLE cards specifically dealt to each player for their use only are said to be 'in the hole'. These cards are dealt face-down so no-one else can see them. See also Hole Cards

Hockey Sticks

♦ ♣ ♥ ♠

HOLE CARD a card dealt face-down to a player – also called a down card. In Hold'em, a player gets dealt two hole cards before the first round of betting starts.

HOOKS a Pair of Jacks.

I

IMPLIED ODDS see pot odds

INSIDE STRAIGHT a hand in which a player needs a card to complete a Straight. For example, the player needs a Five to make a Straight from Three to Seven. See also gutshot

J

JACKSON FIVE a starting hand of Jack-Five (J-5), also known as Motown.

JOKER a wild card with a pre-agreed purpose or value, often an Ace, added to the main 52-card deck.

Jackson Five

K

KAMIKAZE most normally used to describe a player who has gone beyond being on tilt and is playing recklessly. Also occasionally used to describe a starting hand of King-King.

KANSAS CITY LOWBALL a variety of Draw Poker in which Aces are high and the best hand is Seven-Five-Four-Three-Two. Flushes and Straights are bad hands. Also known as Deuce-to-Seven Lowball.

KICKER the highest card not used in the main part of a hand. For example, a hand of King-Jack-Jack-Seven-Four is a Pair of Jacks with a King kicker. If another player has a Pair of Jacks, the hand will be decided by the highest kicker.

KILL an enforced blind, often double the size of the big blind, sometimes required when a player has won two pots in a row. Also known as killing the pot and kill blind.

KILL BLIND see Kill

KILL BUTTON a disc indicating a player who has won two pots in a row.

KOJAK hole cards of King-Jack (K-J).

Kojak

L

LADIES a Pair of Queens, also known as Hilton Sisters or Siegfried and Roy.

LADY a single Queen.

LATE POSITION a player who gets to act late in a round. An advantageous position, as few can raise behind and other players' decisions have been made.

LEG UP a term used for having won the previous pot.

LIMIT POKER a game with limits on betting, also known as fixed-limit poker.

LIMP IN a play done from late position, usually pre-flop, and only calling the big blind. Normally done with mid-strength hands that

♦ ♣ ♥ ♠

would certainly be mucked in an earlier position as too many players would be able to act after the call and raise it.

Little Slick

LITTLE SLICK a starting hand of Ace-Queen.

LIVE ONE as in 'we've got a live one here', used to describe a player who plays far too many hands looking for action.

LOCK–UP a chip that reserves a seat for a player.

LONGSHOT when something has very little chance of happening. If a player needs a specific card to win the pot, they are on a longshot.

LOOSE a player who plays loosely plays a lot of hands.

LOOSE GAME a game in which most of the players play lots of hands.

LOWBALL a variety of Draw Poker where the lowest hand wins the pot.

LOW CARD the lowest upcard dealt in Seven-Card Stud.

M

MECHANIC a cheat who shuffles the deck to give himself a winning hand.

MIDDLE PAIR when the second highest community card on the board is paired.

MISCALL the inaccurate verbal description of a hand.

Mommas and Poppas

MISDEAL when a deal has been performed incorrectly, resulting in a reshuffle and new deal.

MOMMAS AND POPPAS two Pairs – one of Kings, one of Queens.

MONSTER a high-scoring hand.

MOTOWN a starting hand of Jack-Five (J-5), also called a Jackson Five.

MTT a multi-table tournament.

MUCK or **MUCK IT** to throw a hand away, to fold a hand.

N

NEWLYWEDS a starting hand of King-Queen.

NICKEL $500 in poker terminology.

NO-LIMIT a game with no betting limits at all.

NUTS the best hand possible, one which cannot be beaten in that particular game.

♦ ♣ ♥ ♠

O

OCTOPUS a Pair of pocket Eights.

OFF-SUIT two cards of different suits, usually used when describing hole cards.

OLDSMOBILE a Hold'em starting hand of Nine-Eight, named after the Oldsmobile 98 car.

Octopus

OMAHA one of the principal varieties of poker. See pages 95–97

OPEN-ENDED a Straight draw that can be completed at either end. For example, with a hand of Five-Six-Seven-Eight, then a Four or a Nine makes the Straight.

OPENER the player who makes the first voluntary bet.

OPTION the opportunity given to a blind to raise a bet.

OUTS the cards that will improve or make a hand. The more outs, the better the odds of winning.

OVERCARD a hole card higher than any cards on the board.

OVERPAIR a pocket Pair that is higher than any possible Pair made with a card from the flop or board.

P

PAIR any two cards of the same value, such as two Twos, or two Queens.

PASS to decline to bet, or to decline to call a bet.

PASSIVE a player that frequently does not bet or raise.

PAT in Draw Poker, to have such a good hand that the player does not need to draw.

PAY–OFF to put more money in the pot by calling a bet or raise when not holding the best hand. The best hand will bet accordingly to get the second best hand to pay him.

PLAY MONEY a game, normally played online, where no money is used. The chips are play money only. Used by those learning the game who do not want to lose money doing so.

PLAYING THE BOARD when the board cards make the hand with no help from a player's own hole cards.

POCKET the hole cards dealt face down in Omaha and Hold'em.

POCKET PAIR Paired hole cards, such as Six-Six.

POCKET ROCKETS a Pair of Aces in the hole. Also known as American Airlines or bullets.

Pocket Rockets

POT all the money bet on a hand forms the pot, and the winner takes it, or the winners share it. When one player is all-in, there can also be further betting between other players which creates a side pot.

POT–LIMIT POKER a game where the largest bet allowed is the size of the pot at that moment. For example, if one player bets $10, and two players call it, the pot size and thus the maximum bet for the next player is $30.

PRE–FLOP part of a game before 'flop' community cards are dealt.

POT ODDS

Pot odds refers to the ratio between the amount of money in the pot and the amount of money that a player must put down in order to call a bet. If, for example, the pot contains $63 and the required bet to stay in the game is $7, then the pot odds are 9:1.

Matt Damon trying hard not to show that he is grappling with the pot odds in *Rounders* (1998).

With some nimble mental arithmetic and a careful appraisal of the information available about other player's hands, you can use the pot odds to work out whether you should call or fold. To continue the example, if the pot odds are 9:1, then you should only call if you think that your chances of holding (or drawing) the best hand are better than 9:1. If you'd rather deal with percentages, this works out as 10%, which is reached by dividing the amount you're putting down ($7) by the total size of the pot, including your bet ($63 + $7 = $70).

Implied odds are a modification of pot odds, whereby the ratio of betting outlay to potential winnings might be improved by an increased pot and/or the likelihood of hitting one's hand as the game proceeds.

Reverse implied odds are a further modification of pot odds, whereby the ratio of betting outlay to potential losses might decrease if the pot does not improve, and one is holding a hand which might be beaten.

♦ ♣ ♥ ♠

Quads

Q

QUADS an alternative term for Four of a Kind, such as four Aces or four Fours.

QUEENTREY a starting hand of a Queen with a Three, also known as a San Francisco Busboy or Gay Waiter.

R

RAGS cards that are rubbish or don't improve the hand.

RAILBIRD a watcher of live poker games rather than a player. So-called as they loiter on the rails around the tables.

RAINBOW a mix of suits; a rainbow flop in Hold'em, for example, could be Hearts, Clubs, Diamonds.

RAISE to increase the size of bet made by a player in earlier position.

RAKE the charge for playing made by a casino or poker room. Either a table fee for the hour – often $5 per player – or a percentage of each pot up to a maximum of $5.

RERAISE to raise further a raise. A very bold move done either when holding a strong hand, or bluffing aggressively.

RING GAME also known as a cash game, where players can cash in and leave when they choose.

RIVER the final community card dealt, also called Fifth Street.

RIVERBOAT a Full House made on the river, the final card in Texas Hold'em.

ROCK a tight player who only plays when he has a very good starting hand.

ROUNDER a working professional who, like a grinder, concentrates on lower-level stakes to make a living.

ROUTE 66 pocket Sixes.

ROYAL FLUSH the top hand, a Straight Flush Ace-King-Queen-Jack-Ten.

Route 66

RUN consecutive cards that create a Straight; Four-Five-Six-Seven-Eight is a run.

RUNNER a card needed to help a player's hand. If you need two cards to help, then you need runner-runner.

S

SAILBOATS pocket Fours.

SANDBAGGING laying a trap with a strong hand to keep others in the pot. Also known as Slowplaying.

SAN FRANCISCO BUSBOY a starting hand of a Queen with a Three, also known as a Queentrey or Gay Waiter.

SATELLITE a tournament where the winners qualify for a much bigger tournament.

SCARE CARD a community card that hits the board which could massively improve an opponent's hand.

SCOOP a term used in high/low split games where a player scoops the whole pot by winning both high and low, or just high when no hand qualifies for low.

SEMI-BLUFF a bet with a weak hand that does, however, have the potential to improve greatly.

SET an alternative term for Three of a Kind, such as three Fours or three Jacks. Also known as Trips.

Set

SEVEN-CARD STUD One of the principal varieties of poker. See page 92

See page 92

SEVENTH STREET in Seven-Card Stud, the seventh and last card to be dealt to each player.

SHARK a good player that seeks out easy games to win money. Sharks, of course, feed on fish.

SHORT BUY when a buy-in is lower than the minimum required.

SHORT STACK a player without many chips left. It is normal for short stack players to make a move by going all-in.

SHOWDOWN the stage of a game when, after the final card is dealt and the final round of betting completed, those left in the pot get to show their cards to determine who is the winner.

SHUFFLE the mixing of the cards before dealing commences.

SIDE POT when a player is all-in, but others with bigger stacks of chips continue betting through the hand, a side pot is made. The all-in player does not win the side pot if he wins the main pot.

SIEGFRIED AND ROY a Pair of pocket Queens, named after the Las Vegas entertainers.

SIT AND GO a tournament where players sit at a single table and the game begins when the allotted seats are filled. Mostly found online.

SIXTH STREET in Seven-Card Stud, the sixth card to be dealt to each player.

SLOWPLAY deliberately underplaying a strong hand; also known as sandbagging.

Siegfried and Roy

SLOW ROLLING taking a long time to show a winning hand. Frowned upon at the table.

SMALL BET in a fixed-limit game, the small bet is the lower of the two bet sizes allowed.

SMALL BLIND the lower of the two compulsory bets, the small blind is immediately to the left of the dealer. See blinds

SNOWMEN a Pair of Eights. Also known as an octopus.

♦ ♣ ♥ ♠

SPLIT POT when the pot is divided between players, usually due to a tie for best hand.

STACK the player's chips.

STEAL THE BLIND a bluff in late position to win the enforced bets.

STEAL THE POT using a bluff to trick others into folding.

STONE COLD NUTS a hand that cannot be beaten.

STRADDLE BET a blind bet made by the person first to act that is double the big blind.

STRAIGHT a hand of five cards of any suit that make a Run, such as Four-Five-Six-Seven-Eight.

STRAIGHT FLUSH a Straight, but all of the same suit, such as Eight-Nine-Ten-Jack-Queen of Spades.

STRING BET when a player puts enough chips onto the baize or in the pot but then increases the bet without clearly raising. It is best practice when raising to announce it verbally: 'Raise'. Verbal commands are binding so, for example, once you say 'I call', that is all you can do.

Straight Flush

STUB that part of the deck which has not been dealt.

STUD one of the principal methods of playing poker, which involves players in constructing their hands out of hole cards and community cards . See pages 90–92

SUITED a term describing two starting cards that are connected and are of the same suit to make suited connectors, for example a Five and a Six of Hearts.

T

TABLE STAKES when only the money or chips on the table at the start of a hand can be bet.

TEXAS HOLD'EM one of the principal varieties of poker. See pages 93-95

THREE OF A KIND three cards in a hand of the same rank, such as three Kings. Also known as trips, or a set.

THREE WISE MEN a hand in poker that has three Kings.

Three Wise Men

♦ ♣ ♥ ♠

TIGHT describes a player who bets little.

TILT when a player reacts angrily to some play, bets recklessly, and loses discipline, they are said to be on tilt. Bad form at the table.

TOP PAIR pairing the highest board card.

TRIPS another term for a set or Three of a Kind, such as three Jacks.

TURN the fourth community card in Hold'em or Omaha.

TWO PAIR A hand with two Pairs and one other card.

U

UNDERPAIR a Pair that is lower than a possible Pair helped by the board, or community cards.

UNDER THE GUN the player to the left of the big blind and who is first to act.

UPCARD used in Stud, an upcard is a card dealt face-up.

W

WAGER a bet.

WHEEL a Straight of Ace-Two-Three-Four-Five – the lowest possible Straight; also known as the Bicycle.

WILD CARD a card that has been designated wild can be used as any rank or suit.

WIRED PAIR a Pair in the hole.

WPT The World Poker Tour.

WSOP The World Series of Poker.

HOW TO
PLAY POKER

THE GAMES
EXPLAINED

A Game of Many Hands

Don't be daunted by the huge variety of poker games. On the whole they all revolve around the same principle – the player with the best five-card poker hand wins (although there are some versions where the worst hand takes the money, but more on that later). This means that poker (in all its forms) is a vying game. The players bet on who holds the best combination of cards, progressively raising the stakes (and thus the value of the pot) until either a showdown occurs, when the player holding the best hand wins the pot, or all but one player have given up betting and folded – dropped out of the game – in which case the remaining player, the last to raise, wins the pot without a showdown.

The major differences between the various forms of poker lie in how the players come by their five-card hands. Some forms have shared community cards (sometimes called board cards) that can be used by all players to improve their hands; in some, players only use the cards dealt directly to them. Some versions of the game force all players to expose a certain number of their cards; in others the entire hand is hidden from opponents. Some styles of poker allow players to pick their best five cards from a choice of seven; in others players can get rid of cards they don't like and are dealt new ones.

Confused? Well don't be. The four games detailed below will give you the platform you need to be able to play all of the hundreds of poker variations that exist. But rest assured, the four main poker games described below, and their common variations, are the ones most frequently played today, both in casinos and online. And once you have grasped these, no version will be beyond you.

♦ ♣ ♥ ♠

DEALING AND SHUFFLING

In a casino you rarely have to worry about dealing and shuffling, as a dealer will usually be supplied. However, for home games it's best that everyone follows some basic rules.

The first and most obvious point is to use an unmarked, preferably new, deck of cards. These should be given a good shuffle before play begins. To avoid cards being seen or manipulated, shuffling should never be done in the hand, in the style of a magician. Instead, shuffle all cards face down, mixing them together on the felt.

How not to shuffle at the poker table. Elaborate handplay such as the 'train' may allow cards to be seen by the players.

Next, place a plastic card or joker on the bottom of the pack to ensure the bottom card is not glimpsed; "burn" or "muck" (discard) the top card and deal the hole cards to the players, one at a time, and in turn.

For every subsequent dealing round, the top card must again be burned. This is to ensure that no player can recognise the next card to be dealt by spotting a mark or scratch on its back.

Continue burning and dealing until the hand is completed. Then move the dealer button one player to the left and shuffle up and deal.

THE WINNING HANDS

It is important before first sitting at a poker table that you understand the basic winning hands. These tend to be common to all forms of poker, with the exception of Lowball, where the lowest hand wins, or High/Low where the pot can be split between the highest and lowest scoring hands (and it is possible to scoop the pot in such a game, by holding a hand that qualifies as both, and is better than anyone else's).

The following winning hands are organized in order of importance or rank.

ROYAL FLUSH a Straight comprising Ace-King-Queen-Jack-Ten, suited. The highest possible hand. An unsuited hand comprising these cards is merely a high Straight.

STRAIGHT FLUSH sometimes called a natural Flush; five cards, all of the same suit, in numerical order. The higher the order, the better the hand.

♦ ♣ ♥ ♠

FOUR OF A KIND fairly self-descriptive, simply four cards of the same rank or value, such as four Aces or four Fives. In the case of two players holding Four of a Kind, the highest rank or value wins.

FULL HOUSE a hand comprising Three of a Kind and a Pair, for instance King-King-King-Three-Three.

FLUSH five cards all of the same suit, but not in any order, such as Five-Three-Eight-Jack-Two of Diamonds.

STRAIGHT five cards in order, but not of the same suit, for example Two Hearts-Three Diamonds-Four Hearts-Five Clubs-Six Spades.

♦ ♣ ♥ ♠

THREE OF A KIND any three cards of
the same rank or value,
obviously in different
suits; the hand may
include any two other
cards but, in the case of
a draw, the highest rank
wins – for instance three
Tens beats three Nines.

TWO PAIR any combination of
two pairs of cards of the
same rank or value,
such as King-King-
Three-Three or
Ten-Ten-Five-Five.
The remaining card
does not contribute to the
hand, unless there is a draw. In this case, the fifth card acts
as a kicker.

ONE PAIR any two
cards of the same
value, such as two
Threes or two Kings.
Again, the remaining
cards in the hand are of
no value except in the case
of a draw, in which the highest card acts as a kicker to determine
the winning hand.

HIGH CARD the lowest possible winning hand. When nobody holds a Pair or better, the winner may be determined simply by the highest card held.

Lowball Winning Hands

These might vary according to which version you are playing, but basically you are looking for the lowest winning hand. Sometimes Aces are both high and low, or either high or low. If

Aces are low, and Straights and Flushes permitted, then Ace-Two-Three-Four-Five is the best hand.

However, in Kansas City Lowball (or Deuce-to-Seven Lowball) the Aces are high, so the best possible winning hand is Two-Three-Four-Five-Seven (the hand excludes the Six, to avoid making a high-scoring Straight). For a fuller examination of Lowball rules and hands see Pitfalls of Lowball, page 89.

THE CAUTIONARY TALE OF GOVERNOR CARNEY

Ensuring that you fully understand the acceptable winning hands in whatever variety of poker you are playing is essential. For the most part, the winning hands described on the previous pages are accepted, but in variations of Lowball things can get tricky. As can games involving wild cards or jokers.

Bear in mind the story of Thomas Carney, a former governor of Kansas in the mid-1860s, who visited Dodge City in 1877 looking to "entice our unsophisticated denizens into the national game of poker" as the local newspaper gleefully recorded. He settled at a table with three local 'businessmen', whom nobody bothered to tell Carney were professional gambling sharks. After several hands, and several drinks, the confident Carney reckoned he was on a winning roll, holding four Kings and an Ace.

At the time, the winning poker hands were evolving. A Flush outranked a Straight, but a Straight Flush, involving five consecutive cards of the same suit, had not been acknowledged as the premier winning hand. In fact, the best hands available were four Aces, or four Kings and an Ace, the latter being completely unbeatable as no-one else could possibly hold four Aces.

However, this evening the game used a 53-card deck, including a joker (or 'cuter') which could be played as an extra Ace. Having chased some vigorous betting, raising at $100 a go, Carney played his hand, assuming the now mountainous pot was his. He stretched out his arm to gather in his prize. But he was in for a shock, as the one remaining player revealed his hand of four Aces, the only possible better hand.

Carney's face fell and, as he withdrew from the saloon, he was heard to mutter 'I forgot about the cuter'. A dazed and broken old man, 'without shirtstuds or other ornament' was described leaving Dodge City on the next day's train.

♦ ♣ ♥ ♠

Jokers and Wild Cards
Though not widely used today, some forms of poker involve a 53-card pack – all the regular cards plus a joker or wild card (sometimes called a cuter).

THE SET-UP OF THE POKER TABLE

The dealer is usually identified by a button, and is selected by a vartiety of methods including a highest-card deal. Direction of play is always clockwise.

For those varieties of poker which involve blinds (enforced bets to establish a pot), the small blind is the player to the left of the dealer, the big blind the player to his or her left. The first person to check, call or raise is the player immediately to the big blind's left – said to be under the gun and in an early position – while the players to the dealer's right are in late position.

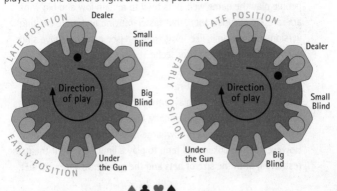

♦ ♣ ♥ ♠

DRAW POKER

Draw poker – in which players are allowed to get rid of cards and draw new ones from the deck – is the version most people first learn when growing up. Yet before the American Civil War it was virtually unheard of. Five-Card Draw rose to prominence in the latter half of the 19th century and it became the most popular version of the game for the next half-century, right up to the outbreak of World War II. It flourished in this period thanks in many ways to the Californian government. In 1910, the US State of Nevada made the running of a betting game a criminal offence, but the Attorney General of California declared that, while Stud poker (see page 90) was a game of chance, Draw poker was a game of skill. The state's gambling laws were hence not applied to it, and people could play it openly and legally.

However, its popularity has seriously waned in the past 50 years and, while it is still not uncommon in home games, it is now rarely played in casinos and is not popular online. It is a slow-moving game with few rounds of betting and winning hands that are invariably low (high cards and Pairs are usually enough). When people play the game well, pots tend to remain low and big wins are rare. No surprise, then, that faster-moving and more exciting versions of the game, like Texas Hold'em (see page 93), have since come to dominate the poker scene.

The Rules of Five-Card Draw

Two to seven people can play, although some websites limit tables to a maximum of five. Traditionally, Five-Card Draw was a no-limit game, meaning no cap on how large raises and reraises could be. However, online poker sites tend to play a limit version of the game, restricting both the size of bets and the number of times the bet can be raised during a round – these will vary depending on where you are playing. Both small and big blinds – enforced bets made by the two players immediately to the left of the dealer respectively – also tend to be employed online to get the betting going. Antes – a small bet placed by all players at the start of the hand – are more common in casinos and in home games.

A plastic dealer button that moves around the table clockwise after each hand is placed in front of a player who becomes nominal dealer for the round. Its starting position can be decided by a number of random methods including a high-card deal. After the blinds or antes are paid, each player is dealt five face-down cards one at a time – there are no communal or face-up cards.

A round of betting follows, with players gambling on the strength of their initial five cards. If antes have been paid, the player next to the dealer is the first to act. If blinds have been paid, it is the player immediately to the left of the big blind who goes first. Anyone can raise the stakes at this stage. Those not wishing to risk their hand can now fold, but anyone who wants to continue must at least call the largest bet, or increase the pot further by reraising. If there are no raises at this stage in a game involving blinds, then anyone wishing to continue to stay in must match the value of the big blind.

If, after all this, more than one player is left, then the draw phase begins. Each player specifies the number of cards he wishes to replace and discards that many from his hand. In some versions the number of cards that can be drawn is limited, but most online games allow you to replace the entire hand. The replacement cards are dealt from those remaining in the deck. A second betting round then occurs. For a player to stay in the hand, he must call any raises.

If a raise is not called, the player who makes the final bet wins the hand and does not have to reveal his cards. If a raise is called, then those players left turn over their cards and the best poker hand wins the pot.

Variations on Draw Poker

LOWBALL played like Five-Card Draw, except with one key difference – the lowest hand wins. Low hands have variable definitions. In Ace-to-Five Lowball, Straights and Flushes do not count, so Ace-Two-Three-Four-Five is the best hand. In Deuce-to-Seven Lowball (also known as Kansas City Lowball) Straights and Flushes do count, and Aces are considered high, so the best hand is Two-Three-Four-Five-Seven unsuited, the Six being omitted to avoid making a Straight.

SPIT IN THE OCEAN played with three to twelve players, the rules and betting are the same as Five-Card Draw except that players are dealt four cards with one face-up community card shared by all. The highest hand wins.

ANACONDA played with four to seven players. Everyone is dealt seven cards followed by a round of betting. Then everyone passes three cards to the player on their left and another round of betting occurs. Players then pass two cards to the their left, followed by another round of betting. Then everyone passes a final single card to their left. Anyone can fold at any point when it is their turn to act. Remaining players discard two cards to make their best five-card hand. The highest hand wins. Also known as Pass the Trash.

JACKS-TO-OPEN, TRIPS-TO-WIN played like Five-Card Draw, but players can only open the betting if they're holding a Pair of Jacks or better in an opening hand. If they have such a hand, they have to open the betting. If nobody can start the betting, all hands are

♦ ♣ ♥ ♠

PITFALLS OF LOWBALL

While there are variations of what qualifies as a low hand in different poker games, the basic idea is always the same: to have a low hand is to have no hand at all. If any of the five cards has a value of Nine or higher, the hand will be disqualified from winning the low pot, as it also will be should it contain a Pair, Three of a Kind or a Full House. This is common to any version of poker involving low pots that you are likely to come across. The differences come in attitudes to Straights, Flushes and Aces.

In most Omaha High/Low and Seven-Card Stud High/Low games – the most common to involve low pots in online poker – Straights and Flushes are ignored and Aces can be low. Indeed Aces now become the most valuable cards when forming a low hand. Here, the best possible low hand is Ace-Two-Three-Four-Five (hence the nickname Ace-to-Five for this version), followed by Ace-Two-Three-Four-Six and so on.

However, there are versions where Straights and Flushes do disqualify a hand from being a low one. These games often view Aces as a high card only, so any hand containing one is disqualified. One version is Deuce-to-Seven, and the best possible hand is Two-Three-Four-Five-Seven. Deuce-to-Seven is usually employed in games where there is no splitting of the pot and only the low hand wins, such as Kansas City Lowball, but there is no reason that it cannot be employed in a split-pot game.

discarded and re-dealt. Once the betting starts, play continues as in Five-Card Draw until the showdown. At this point, anyone with Three of a Kind or better must reveal their hand, and the best revealed hand wins the pot. When nobody reveals a hand (meaning nobody has at least Three of a Kind) the draw and betting process is repeated until someone does.

STUD POKER

Stud poker – in which some cards in each player's hand are dealt face-up so the entire table can see – first appeared during the American Civil War, during which a five-card version of the game started to become popular. It was, however, considered too much of a game of chance by the legislating powers in America, and was made illegal as a result. This kept the game in the shadows until the US State of Nevada legalized gambling in 1931, and casinos started to become established.

It still took time for Stud poker to overtake Draw poker in the popularity stakes, and it was the seven-card version of the game that finally, by the time of the outbreak of World War II, had gained the upper hand, so to speak. As Las Vegas began to thrive in the post-war years, so did Seven-Card Stud and, for 40 years, it was the poker players' game of choice. Although no longer number one, it's still a popular game both online and in casinos.

The Rules of Seven-Card Stud

Two to eight people are needed for a game. Seven-Card Stud tends to involve bet limits. These will vary depending where you are playing and, in tournament play, will increase at regular intervals as the game progresses. For the purposes of this explanation the low limit is $1 and the high limit $2.

Before any cards are dealt, each player pays a small ante into the pot – usually about one-fifth of the low limit, so in this case 20 cents. Everyone is then dealt three cards, the first two face-down and the third face-up. The player with the lowest face-up card has to bring in. This means he must place an enforced bet – at least half the low limit bet, but it can be the value of the high limit if

♦ ♣ ♥ ♠

the player likes his cards. The betting then goes around the table in a clockwise direction and players can fold, call the existing bet or raise. If there are any raises, all players wishing to continue to the next stage must call that bet.

Those left after this round of betting (assuming there is more than one) are dealt a fourth face-up card and another round of betting follows. The player with the highest hand from their two cards showing (the very highest being a Pair of Aces) is the first to act. Another card is dealt face-up to all remaining players followed by another round of betting. From this point forward the player with the best three cards showing (the best possible hand being three Aces) is the first to act, and all bets and raises must be equal to the high limit bet size.

If more than one player remains, the sixth card is dealt face-up and there is another round of betting at the high limit. If there is still more than one player involved after this, a seventh card is dealt, this time face-down. The final round of betting follows. Those players still in must turn their cards over and the one with the best five-card poker hand wins.

Variants on Stud Poker

FIVE-CARD STUD played by two to ten people with similar rules to the Seven-Card version. All players pay an ante and are then dealt two cards – one face down the other face up. The player with the lowest face-up card starts betting with a bring-in. This is followed by a third, fourth and fifth face-up card, each followed by a round of betting. The highest poker hand wins.

♦ ♣ ♥ ♠

SEVEN-CARD STUD HIGH/LOW played exactly the same way as Seven-Card Stud, except that the pot is split evenly between the highest and lowest hands. To qualify for the low half of the pot, the hand must contain five cards no higher than an eight. Ace plays both high and low, while Straights and Flushes do not count for the low hand. The best possible low hand is thus Ace-Two-Three-Four-Five or the bicycle.

RAZZ the same rules as Seven-Card Stud, except that only the low hand wins. The bring-in is required from the player with the highest card on show, and the lowest displayed hand acts first on all betting rounds. Again, Flushes and Straights do not count, so Ace-Two-Three-Four-Five is the best possible hand.

CARIBBEAN STUD a version of Five-Card Stud played on a Blackjack-sized table in casinos and against the house. All players pay an ante and are dealt five cards face-down. The dealer hand is dealt with the first four cards down and the last one up. Players then either fold or stay in, with a bet that is double the price of the ante. If the dealer does not have at least an Ace-King combination, then the player wins even money on the ante and the double-the-ante bet is returned. If the dealer does hold an Ace-King, then the hands are compared and if the player has the higher hand, he wins even money on the ante and then a variety of odds on his larger bet, depending on what his hand is. For instance, Three of a Kind pays 3:1, a Full House 7:1 and a Royal Flush 100:1.

♦ ♣ ♥ ♠

TEXAS HOLD'EM

Texas Hold'em, dubbed the 'Cadillac of Poker', is now by far the most popular version of the game, and is played by millions around the world. Its rise to the top of the poker tree started in the 1970s when the World Series of Poker began in Las Vegas using the No-Limit Texas Hold'em tournament as its flagship event. Being the fastest-moving and most exciting version of poker, Texas Hold'em was undoubtedly the catalyst for the online poker explosion that started in the 1990s and continues to this day. The game has even managed to become a regular fixture in television schedules around the globe, with many countries now dedicating entire channels to round-the-clock poker coverage.

Yet, despite Texas Hold'em's modern ubiquity, very little is known about its roots. It appears to be related to Seven-Card Stud in that players make their best five-card hand from seven available cards. The name would suggest a Texan birth, and legend does proclaim it to have started in Robstown, Texas in 1900 from where it is supposed to have reached the state capital Dallas by 1925. However, nobody knows for sure where, when, and by whom the first Texas Hold'em game was played.

The Rules of No-Limit Texas Hold'em

Two to ten people are needed for a single table. A plastic dealer button that moves around the table clockwise after each hand is placed in front of a player who becomes nominal dealer for the round. Its starting position can be decided by a number of random methods including a high-card deal.

The player immediately to the left of the dealer button places an enforced small blind bet. The player immediately to the left of him (two places from the dealer button) places an enforced big blind bet twice the value of the small. In tournament play, the value of these blinds will increase at regular intervals. Once the blinds have been paid, each player is dealt two cards face-down, one at a time. Then a round of betting occurs, starting with the player immediately to the left of the big blind, who is said to be under the gun. For a player to stay in he must either call the value of the big blind, raise it (usually by at least the same value again) or fold. In No-Limit Texas Hold'em the only factor limiting the upper value of any bet is the number of chips a player possesses, and they can go all-in (that is, bet their entire chip stack) during any round of the betting.

If there is more than one player left after this first round of betting, three face-up community cards are dealt. This is called the flop and is followed by another round of betting. All betting from this point on is started by the player immediately to the left of the dealer button. Any raises must be called by other players for the fourth community card to be shown. This is known as the turn, or Fourth Street, and leads to another round of betting. If more than one player still remains after this, the last of the five face-up community cards – called the river or Fifth Street – is dealt, followed by the final round of betting. Any remaining players at this stage enter a showdown, where the players' two face-down cards are turned over. The player with the highest five-card poker hand from the seven available cards wins the pot. If a player wins the pot at any time from an uncalled bet, they are under no obligation to reveal their cards, but can do so if they choose.

♦ ♣ ♥ ♠

Variations on Texas Hold'em

LIMIT TEXAS HOLD'EM also known just as Texas Hold'em, so check before you start to play. Exactly the same as No-Limit Texas Hold'em except for the restrictions placed on betting. A minimum and maximum bet are imposed and, on any given round, players may only raise a fixed number of times, usually four.

POT-LIMIT TEXAS HOLD'EM again the only difference is in the betting restrictions. The maximum raise any player can make during any round of betting is the total of the active pot. This includes all bets on the table plus the amount that the active player must first call before raising.

OMAHA

Much like its close cousin Texas Hold'em, the origins of Omaha (often called Omaha Hold'em) are shrouded in mystery. Poker player and writer Lou Krieger believes the game was "invented by Hold'em players who figured that with four cards to start with, each player would be capable of playing many more hands, resulting in more action and bigger hands". As Omaha players have nine cards with which to make a five-card hand, the chances of big hands are indeed greatly increased, although it does make for a much more complex game. Omaha, along with its variant Omaha High/Low, has developed into a very popular online game.

The Rules of Omaha

Two to ten people are needed for a single table. Omaha involves bet limits, and these will vary depending where you are playing: in tournament play, these will increase at regular intervals. For the purposes of this explanation the low limit is $1 and the high limit $2.

A plastic dealer button, that is moved around the table clockwise after each hand, is placed in front of the player who becomes nominal dealer for the round. Its starting position can be decided by a number of random methods, including a high-card deal. The player immediately to the left of the dealer button places an enforced small blind bet, usually half the minimum bet, so in this case 50 cents. The player immediately to the left of him (two places from the dealer button) places an enforced big blind bet, usually the full value of the minimum bet, in this case $1. In tournament play, the value of these blinds, along with the value of the bet limits, will increase at regular intervals.

Once the blinds have been paid, each player is dealt four cards face down one at a time. It should be noted here that only two of these cards can be used to make the final five-card poker hand. A round of betting follows this deal, with the player next to the big blind the first to act. For a player to stay in he must either call the value of the big blind ($1), raise it (by a maximum of $2 in this case), or fold. Usually only four raises are allowed per round of betting.

Following this comes the flop – three community or board cards dealt face-up in the centre of the table. From this point on the player to the left of the dealer button is always the first to act. Bets are at the minimum level at this stage (in our case $1). Then follows the fourth community card, called the turn, or Fourth Street, followed by a round of betting at the maximum level (in our case $2). Finally the last community card, the river, or Fifth Street, is dealt, followed by another round of betting at the maximum level. Those still in at this stage turn their cards over. The player with the best hand, combining two of the four cards they were dealt with three of the community cards, wins the pot.

♦ ♣ ♥ ♠

Variations on Omaha

POT-LIMIT OMAHA this game works the same way as Omaha, except that the maximum raise any player can make during any round of betting is the total of the active pot. This includes all bets on the table, plus the amount that the active player must first call before raising.

OMAHA HIGH/LOW played exactly the same way as Omaha, except that the pot is split between the highest and lowest hands if a hand qualifies for the low pot. To qualify for the low half, the hand must contain five cards no higher than an Eight. Ace plays both high and low, while Straights and Flushes do not count for the low hand. The best possible low hand therefore is Ace-Two-Three-Four-Five.

Now, you should be able to take on any variety or style of poker played today. But remember – check what the winning hands are, what the betting limits (if any) are, and stay cool.

POKER STRATEGY

It's All in the Planning

Success at poker is all about strategy. If you haven't got one, you might as well spend your money on lottery tickets or roulette. Although luck naturally plays a part in poker, skill is more important – that's why good players win money consistently. Part of that skill is about managing your luck. And successfully managed luck means winning money, which is the name of the game. While this guide to your strategic options isn't exhaustive – indeed it can take a lifetime to master all the nuances of the different forms of poker – it should point you in the right direction. To begin with, this advice is true of most forms of poker, except where indicated, but most strategic advise is based on which form of poker you are playing. The following notes focus on the key strategic considerations.

Position

Your position in relation to the first bet (fixed in Hold'em and Omaha, changeable in Seven-Card Stud) has a big influence on which cards you should play. If you are in an early betting position, you will be committing money to the pot without having had any indication of the strength of other player's hands. In this position, you need to be careful, and you'd be unwise to play with marginal hands, as there is a big risk you'll run into a raise, and be forced to either fold or play against a starting hand that is clearly stronger and more likely to win.

However, in a late position – the further on in the betting order you are – the more of an indication you have of the strength of your opponents' hands. If, for example, you're 'on the button' in Hold'em – you are the nominal dealer and thus the last to bet – and nobody has raised by the time the betting reaches you, you're in a position to call the blind with a marginal hand, which is called limping in: by

♦ ♣ ♥ ♠

raising, you might steal the blind. This is not a hard and fast rule, and depends on the size of the blind – in tournament play this can become very expensive. You also need to be wary of opponents who might be slow-playing a big hand – a common tactic used to suck more people into the pot. But on the whole, marginal hands, particularly ones that play better against a large number of opponents (as they are also likely to be holding marginal hands), become more playable when there have been no raises and you are among the last to bet.

Starting Hands

Anyone learning any form of poker must learn which hands to play and which to fold. Most beginners want to be involved as often as possible and will play terrible hands just so that they can see the flop. They have little or no strategy and, while they may get lucky a few times, they will soon be losing money. The truth is that most hands should be folded. The top players play very few hands – and that's because the majority of hands are weak. You have to know how to spot a strong hand, a hand which has the potential to make a winning hand. Potentially strong opening hands are detailed below – as are seemingly strong but potentially weak ones.

SEVEN-CARD STUD

The positional considerations of Texas Hold'em and Omaha differ with Seven-Card Stud, mainly because the player with whom the betting starts changes, depending on the cards on show (although being last can still be an advantage).

It is the exposed cards that hold the key to playing this game well. It is important that you take note of the cards on show, and that you remember the ones that have been folded. These cards affect your odds of making a hand, help you figure out what other players are holding or chasing, and enable you to make sensible decisions about playing on or folding. All other players will be memorizing those cards that have been exposed – and if you don't, you're at a serious disadvantage.

Starting Hands

ROLLED-UP TRIPS a set of Aces is the best possible starting hand, but any set (Three of a Kind) is worth playing. Smaller trips need to be played aggressively to discourage others chasing Straights, Flushes or higher trips from playing. Higher trips can be played slowly to draw others into playing.

HIGH PAIRS these are next best behind rolled-up trips, but need to be aggressively played to discourage those drawing to a Flush or a Straight from playing. If you're playing with medium or low Pairs, make sure you have a high kicker. But regardless of the kicker, if you're playing low Pairs after a raise, you're probably best off folding.

THREE CARDS TO A FLUSH play these hands if they are live, that is there are no or very few exposed cards of the suit you need in other hands. Don't raise, however, as the hand in itself is not strong yet, and there's every chance you won't make the Flush and, if you do, you'll want as many people in the pot as possible. Betting will scare them off.

♦ ♣ ♥ ♠

THREE CARDS TO A STRAIGHT again, play
only if live – if there are no or very few
exposed Nines and Kings, for example. Don't
raise, however, as the hand in itself is not
strong yet. Also be aware that a Straight will
lose to a Flush, so if an opponent is drawing

to a Flush and you both get your hands, you'll lose. Avoid chasing a
low Straight, so don't play anything less than Eight-Nine-Ten.

Playing in Subsequent Rounds
The fact that the number of exposed cards varies from hand to
hand makes working out your odds in Seven-Card Stud much more
complicated than in Texas Hold'em, and it will be almost impossible
for the average player to work out to any degree of precision. Use
your intuition and the information available to you, including
cards that are or have been exposed, and the betting behaviour of
other players.

SEVEN-CARD STUD HIGH/LOW
The principles that apply in Seven-Card Stud with respect to exposed
cards and live cards also apply here. However, in this version you are
looking to scoop the entire pot at the risk of losing half of it to a
low hand, so the hands you are trying to get, and thus the starting
cards that are good to play with, are very different indeed. Ideally,
you want cards that are a good start to giving you both a high and
a low hand. As in Omaha High/Low, the value of an Ace as both the
highest and lowest possible card is massive, and in low pots, Flushes
and Straights do not disqualify you from winning (see The Pitfalls of
Lowball, page 89)

♦ ♣ ♥ ♠

Starting Hands

TWO ACES WITH A LOW CARD this is a
good position to win both high and low
pots.

ACE WITH TWO LOW CARDS, ALL SUITED
this has a good shot at making a Flush
and is also well set for a low hand.

THREE CARDS TO A SMALL STRAIGHT well-
placed to land a Straight and scoop the
high pot. The same hand will be well set
for the low pot too.

THREE CARDS TO A SMALL FLUSH a low
Flush can win both the high and
low pots.

ROLLED UP TRIPS this won't make a low
hand but as this puts you in such a strong
position for the high hand, you still have
good odds of scooping the pot.

ANY THREE LOW CARDS these will put you
in a good position for the low half of the
pot, but beware of any exposed Aces, as
anyone with these may be in a stronger
position.

tendency to treat Ace-King like a Pair of Aces, but it's nothing like as valuable – in fact, you'll only flop an Ace or a King and turn it into a strong hand one third of the time.

BIG UNSUITED CARDS these offer good potential for big Pairs but the odds of hitting a Flush are all but negated.

SMALL PAIRS almost every card becomes an overcard with these, so you will be hoping to make a set (Three of a Kind) on the flop to have any chance of winning. As you're not in a strong position from the start, raising or following a raise is a bad idea and, if you don't flop a set, fold to any raises.

ACES WITH LOW KICKERS again, these may look good to an inexperienced player but can get you in a lot of trouble. They are playable, but need to be handled with care. The strength of the kicker is important here – a weak kicker, even if you flop a Pair of Aces, could still be beaten by another player with an Ace hole card, but a stronger kicker.

After the Flop

If you have gone into the flop with a big Pair, you need to be wary of overcards as well as Straight and Flush potential. If someone hits the right cards, even a Pair of Aces can easily be beaten.

Mos[...] her hands will usually need something from the flop to put them [...] a winning position. If this comes, and the player feels he is in an[...] assailable position, it is wise to check and induce a bluff from a p[...] er with a weak hand. If you do get a raise, you can then reraise, a m[...] ve known as a check-raise.

If you flop a [...] nd that is still in danger of being bettered on the turn or river, a[...] early raise is recommended to discourage those on Flush draws, Straight draws or similar.

If you have an incomplete hand at the flop, like a Flush draw (for example, four Club cards that require only one more to make a Flush) you have to work out how many outs – how many cards there are left that can give you a hand – there are remaining. This will give you your odds of hitting a hand. Understanding the relationship between these odds and the money you can win from the pot is the essence of pot odds. If the odds of making your hand are 3-1 and the bet is only one-fifth of the pot, it's usually worth taking the risk.

OMAHA

Starting Hands

Although Omaha is a close relative of Texas Hold'em, the starting hands must be played in an entirely different way. Every Omaha player is dealt four cards, but only two of these can be used to make the hand, and to have the best odds of having a strong hand after the flop, you need to have cards that all work together. There is a total of six two-card combinations possible from the four cards,

'It' girl Clara Bow strategically displays her prowess at winking, and a suited Royal Flush.

and all of these need to be good hands in their own right. Just one dangler (a card that doesn't work with the other three) in your four cards will reduce the playable combinations by half and should in most circumstances (but not all) result in a fold.

Consider the hand King-King-Eight-Five: it does contain the second best two-card hand possible, but that is the only strong two-card combination out of the possible six. King-Eight and King-Five are weak and Eight-Five isn't worth talking about.

Playable Omaha starting hands include:

FOUR HIGH CARDS, DOUBLE-SUITED these hands contain connecting cards, so there is high potential for a big Straight, Flushes and Full Houses. Omaha, unlike Hold'em, is a game where such hands are the norm, and you want starting hands that support their construction.

FOUR CARDS TO A STRAIGHT WITH NO MORE THAN TWO GAPS strong potentials for a high Straight – but beware: if the board Pairs (for example, two Kings in the community cards) or three cards in the same suit come down, you are vulnerable to a Full House and a Flush from elsewhere.

TWO PAIR, AS LONG AS BOTH ARE EIGHT OR HIGHER Pairs less than Eight can get you in trouble as, while they may give you a Full House, in Omaha it's not uncommon for low Full Houses to be beaten by higher ones (something that is very rare in Hold'em). Pairs need to be high, and preferably suited, to be played.

ACE-KING DOUBLE-SUITED TO TWO
SMALLER CARDS a very playable hand, as
it has within it a number of options for a
very high Flush and also the potential for
the highest Straight.

After the Flop

As the winning hands in Omaha are usually very high, you need to flop something big, or at least have a draw to a big hand with many outs, to continue playing. Even very big hands pre-flop can be scuppered if the first three community cards don't fit – Ace Clubs-Ace Diamonds-Queen Diamonds, flopping Three Hearts-Five Spades-Eight Hearts becomes weak.

If a Pair is dealt among the community cards there is a strong possibility of at least one player having a Full House, and if it's not you, you could be in trouble.

There are times in Omaha when you're on a Straight draw with more chance of hitting it than missing it. If you play Ace Spades-Jack Spades-King Diamonds-Ten Spades and flop Eight Spades-Nine Spades-Four Diamonds there are potentially four Sevens, four Queens and eight Spades outs in the deck that can give you a hand. This is well worth playing. But remember, you have not made your Spade Flush in the flop as you can only use two of the hole cards in your hand.

♦ ♣ ♥ ♠

OMAHA HIGH/LOW

Starting Hands

The fact that a pot is split between the highest and the lowest qualifying hand may seem a minor alteration to regular Omaha, but it utterly changes the value of certain starting hands. Don't fall into the trap of trying to just win half of the pot – you should be setting out to scoop both, and to do this you have to select the right hands from the outset.

Aces have a special value in high/low games because they represent both the highest and the lowest cards – and many people won't play an Omaha high/low hand unless they are dealt one. The best Omaha hands are:

A SUITED ACE WITH THREE LOW CARDS
you stand to make an Ace Flush or a
Straight, standing you in good stead to
win the high pot, and no one will be in a
better position to win the low pot should
low cards come in the flop.

ACE-KING, DOUBLE-SUITED this
particular hand offers two Flush
combinations, Straight possibilities, and
two cards to a good low hand.

PAIR OF ACES WITH TWO LOW CARDS
this is a very strong hand, and even
stronger when one or both the Aces
are suited.

PAIR OF ACES AND PAIR OF KINGS,
DOUBLE-SUITED no hope in the low pot,
but very well set for the high. In fact,
any four big cards can be worth playing.

ACE, DEUCE any hand with an Ace and a
Two is worth playing.

ACE-THREE, AS LONG AS THE ACE IS SUITED
only someone holding Ace-Two is in a
stronger position with regards the low
pot. The suited Ace provides a chance
for the high pot after the flop.

ACE-THREE, ACCOMPANIED BY TWO CARDS
GREATER THAN A TEN this is playable,
even if the Ace is not suited.

A SUITED ACE WITH ANY TWO CARDS ABOVE
TEN a strong hand in relation to the high pot,
with potential to win the low.

After the Flop

As in Omaha, the number of cards available
to each player makes competition very stiff
so, unless you are strong after the flop, fold. Remember,
though, that if you're holding Ace-Deuce and three low cards come
in the flop that don't Pair either of yours, nobody can beat you for
the low hand.

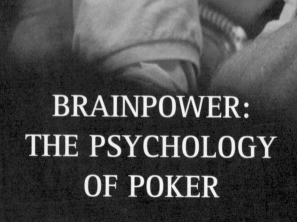

BRAINPOWER:
THE PSYCHOLOGY
OF POKER

Know Thyself and Thus One Will Know Others

Psychology in poker is really no different to the psychology of
human behaviour in any field. It is an attempt to fully comprehend,
predict, and to some extent control, the actions and behaviour
of the other players. In this, a gnarled old poker veteran trying
to increase his hourly rate at the felt is using techniques similar
to those used by shopping malls and retailers desperate to
increase the dollar or pound spend of every shopper on a trip. The
significant difference is that big business combines the wisdom
of thought-police consultants with acres of market research and
shopping-pattern analyses. The poker player must rely on his or her
experience, ability to rapidly comprehend patterns of behaviour at
the table, and a finely honed instinct.

> *"Always remember, the first thing a gambler
> has to do is make friends with himself. A lot
> of people go through this world thinking
> they're someone else. There are a lot of people
> sitting at this table with mistaken identities."*

PUGGY PEARSON QUOTED IN JON BRADSHAW'S *FAST COMPANY* 1975

The dominant popular belief, held by the newer players' devotion to
the power of the myth of bluffing, is that understanding the others
round the table is the most important single thing. But really it is
vital that players fully know themselves. What kind of a personality
are they? Why do they play? What is their natural tempo and style?
And what discipline levels do they have? Because these are the signs
that every other (good) player will also be looking to ascertain and
take advantage of.

♦ ♣ ♥ ♠

Psychology at the table does indeed involve the ability to bluff, and to study the behaviour of those around the baize with chips stacked in front of them, but it must start with self-analysis and, further, a basic understanding of how people behave in groups when they're under pressure, when they're losing, and when they're winning.

Obviously, this must be balanced with cool mental arithmetic. But there are many players who fully understand the subtleties of poker mathematics, who have memorized the cards played, calculated the pot odds and percentages, and yet still remain bad players. This is because, despite knowing the statistics, they have not mastered those other skills needed at the table.

Humans, like dogs, are essentially pack animals with a genetically-blueprinted sense of hierarchy. Successful poker players, however, prefer to be characterized as sharks, admiring the lone predator image, conveniently forgetting that sharks too frequently cruise, hunt and feed in large groups. The fact is that our actions and behaviour are, as often as not, decided not by us but by the group of people around us, as we naturally assume the behaviour of the majority.

At the poker table this conformity can mean that a normally tight player suddenly plays more hands and calls more bets than usual when they find themselves on a very loose table dominated by action players.

Alternatively, towards the end of a tournament or at a sit and go table, when the remaining players are close to the money spots, they will often become more passive, refusing to risk chips and their position in the potential winning stakes. Outstanding players like Stu Ungar knew this, and would regularly dictate play as the

♦ ♣ ♥ ♠

final table approached, raising blinds with poor hands and stealing pots through unashamed aggression. They were rarely challenged, as others remained timid and cautious. Of course, players that did survive such aggressive tactics were then at a huge disadvantage as Ungar usually had a formidably massive chip lead. Even though frequently remarked, this behaviour is still seen at almost every large tournament. This passivity is considered social loafing.

In addition, we are habitually inclined to be rather lenient on ourselves when examining our motivation and judgement in most things we do. So, although we are quick to attribute mistakes that others make to failings in their character or skills, when we suffer the same fate, the reason has to be external factors, most typically attributed to bad luck, for instance. This is known as the fundamental attribution error, and is more simply described as a person desperately trying to find something or someone else to blame rather than facing reality.

Studying Your Opponents

Both the greats from yesteryear as well as new guns like Daniel Negreanu all believe that bluffing is overrated in poker. What they consider to be of more value is watching other players' betting habits. If we accept that a bluff is just a way of fooling the opponent into doing something that is not in their interests, then we should surely spend a lot of time analyzing the opponent. The most prominent facet of their playing is their betting. How do they bet and when? How do they react when called? Do they fold when raised or reraised? In short, what we have to learn and hone is a skill of 'reading hands': understanding what the other player is holding by their betting, and what they **were** holding in previous hands.

♦ ♣ ♥ ♠

It is also important to understand what the other player is thinking.
One way professionals intimidate new or amateur players is by
taking a long time to muck a hand when they have been called;
in those quiet minutes they pressure the caller by staring at him,
making as if to call and generally giving the impression that they are
seriously considering staying in the pot.

> *"He's a good enough player to know that I*
> *know what he's thinkin', just like he knows*
> *what I'm thinkin'. Hell, we're environment, we*
> *know each other like hills and streams."*

PUG PEARSON, FROM JON BRADSHAW'S *FAST COMPANY* (1975)

Frequently, experienced players will know, once called, that they
are going to fold, but they spend the decision minutes unnerving
the opposition, with the effect that their opponents become more
reluctant to semi-bluff or challenge the professional in later hands.
What they are trying to do is control other players' reactions.

Players must study every other player and build up a mental fact-file
about them, their style of play, their habits and physical reactions
and so on, and once these are known the player can then seek
out discrepancies or weaknesses. For example, if a player bets in a
certain manner, placing the chips neatly forward, is then called and
shows a low Pair, then you need to find out if, whether every time
they bet neatly, they are in fact weak. That is why, strategically, it
is sometimes better to call and find out a tell, even if you lose that
particular pot. The information learned should be of benefit in the
long run. If your opponent splashes his chips into the pot later, the
chances are they are strong, allowing you to fold easily.

Self-knowledge, and consequently self-control, is that most elusive of goals. Quite how one achieves it is the domain of endless self-improvement books which clutter publishers' warehouses.

Despite his impressive chipstack, Greg 'Fossilman' Raymer's intimidating shades, large Coke and bored, if not threatening, expression and body language mean are all sending out a wide variety of messages to his fellow players.

However one achieves it, at least a basic contemplation of why one is in the game (is it for fun, is it for money, is it for kudos, is it for the sheer competition?) is an important step in mastering the psychology of poker, because if you don't know why you are playing, you will inevitably be sending out signals to experienced players who will make the most of them.

> *"You can tell by the way they move their checks. You get the reaction, the conversation... watch the veins in his neck, watch his eyes, the way he sweats."*

JOHNNY MOSS, QUOTED IN JON BRADSHAW'S *FAST COMPANY* (1975)

Bluffing

Good players scrutinize every aspect of an opponent: their hands, eyes, the pulse in the neck, their sweat and posture before deciding whether they have the winning hand or are simply bluffing. For all the dramatic allure of flinty-eyed cardsharps using every trick in the book – including deceit – bluffing is a less important part of poker than received wisdom would have it. However, the tactic is used and, more than mere panache, it is a varied and complex skill.

Bluffing, to be done successfully, needs to be allied to a much greater knowledge of the various games of poker themselves, and to understanding the value of the cards – and thus an understanding of the pot odds. It should therefore be used with caution.

So forget the stereotyped images created by Hollywood, dismiss the hype, and start thinking of bluffing as a tool to help you either to maximize profits, or to minimize losses.

TELLS

Here are some of the more useful tells to bear in mind when assessing your fellow players' behaviour.

THE HANDS HAVE IT look out for shaking hands when betting. With newer players this normally means excitement because they have a big hand. It is reverse nerves – they are not nervous because they think they are going to lose, but are excited that they might win.

EYES DOWN an involuntary glance at their chips just after the flop usually means a player has hit their hand. In contrast, prolonged staring at the flop – desperately searching for something – means they missed. Watch out for a bluff here.

THE CHIPS ARE IN watch what chips other players bet with. Large denomination chips often subconsciously indicate strength and confidence, whereas the same size bet but in small denomination chips suggests weakness or a bluff.

FROZEN MOMENT an inadvertent sign of increased tension. Gum chewers at the table will typically stop chewing when they bluff. A similar tell is when a person holds their breath while making their play.

TALKING THE TALK when holding a strong hand players tend to be confident, affable, talkative and relaxed. Agitated behaviour or stilted, broken conversation suggests weakness.

I'M IN an eagerness to bet can reveal a lot. A key tell is if a player usually waits, pondering before calling, but then uncharacteristically bets quickly. It is then likely they have a strong hand. Alternatively, taking your time to act can disguise a multitude of ruses, and is definitely unsettling for the rest of the table.

♦ ♣ ♥ ♠

What do you look for? When do you look for it? And, if you are going to bluff, how do you do it? These are the main questions to keep in mind. Some of the answers lie in the art of reading 'tells'.

Tells

The supposedly giveaway signs – tells – allow you to read your fellow players. Tells remain one of the most glamourous, and glamourised, aspects of poker. The power of getting a read on an opponent so that, despite their cards being face-down, you pretty much know what they are holding, is enormously compelling and empowering if you read the signs correctly. And body language is the key.

The old adage has it that if a player is projecting strength he is bluffing, and if he feigns weakness he is strong. Got that? Well, most other poker players have got that too, and most experienced players are also good at acting – it's one of the important skills at the table.

So, when a player puts a big bet into the pot, leans forward dominantly, and stares straight at you as you contemplate whether to call or fold, the chances are they are bluffing – or are they? Similarly, when a player bets into a pot dismissively and then leans back, eyes scanning round the room with an air of indifference, the chances are they have the nuts – or do they? Don't be taken in. You need to look beyond the obvious.

Basically, as we all know, bluffing is subterfuge, but the fact is that people are creatures of habit. To interpret tells usefully you need to compile a mental dossier on how each player behaves. It is not what they are trying to project, but what they don't know that they are doing that is important. What should emerge from your dossier is the knowledge that they do certain things depending on whether they are bluffing or not.

Doyle Brunson observed that people who chew gum at the table will frequently stop chewing when bluffing. Another tell is how players put their chips, and, more particularly, which chips they put, in the pot. If they use big denominations they are being bold and confident, but a stack of small-value chips is is likely to be a sign of subconscious weakness.

Of course, now everyone knows these little tricks they can set traps which is why out-and-out bluffs are very rare.

Bluff or Semi-Bluff?

Bluffing in early position should rarely be done, as the number of potential callers almost guarantees one other player, intentionally or not, will call your bluff. Even worse, your bluff may be raised, and then you have little option but to muck your hand. So bluffing is frequently done in late position, especially as a late player tries to steal the blinds. Winning blinds is vital, as it protects a chip stack and stops a player effectively being anteed away.

But what is more common, and indeed recommended by such giants of the game as Brunson, is to bluff mostly when you also have a good chance of drawing a card and making a hand.

A straight bluff can only truly work when the opponent folds, and therefore is best used when only one other player is in the pot. A straight bluff will rarely work if there are more than two players in the pot because they may be getting pot odds to stay in, may actually have a hand, or may be drawing to a hand. In this situation, a semi-bluff should be used.

If you call a bet with a hand that needs to draw to be made, then you have to figure out the pot odds and judge whether it is worth

The 'bling' factor: whether or not it is a good idea to demonstrate your wealth and success at the table is a moot point. It can intimidate quite successfully, but also make you a prize target.

calling. This is simple mathematics: if, for example, the odds of drawing the card for your Flush is 6:1 and the pot odds are more than this, then it is worth calling. This, if you bet, is a semi-bluff. In other words, you have more than one way to win the hand, and are not entirely relying on the success of your bluff..

Of course, your opponent could fold, allowing you to win, or they could call and then you could make your hand on the next card. Poker players term this leaving oneself 'outs', which means you can still win the pot with the best hand if it comes to a showdown.

If, however, you are against a player that you are sure will call, then there is no chance of a semi-bluff because they probably will not fold. Then you have to reckon your pot odds to decide whether you are getting value to call.

In fact the semi-bluff, rather than the full bluff, requires more subtlety, a more careful balance of observation, behavioural knowledge and mental arithmetic (in essence, a combination of all the key factors) than the classic Hollywood showdown. And it will gain you more in the long run.

So, to sum up, it is a combination of self-awareness, observation and mathematics that should determine whether you use the ultimate psychological poker gambit – the bluff. Setting this aside, however, the importance of psychology, in terms of understanding how and why you yourself play, and as far as possible manipulating how others at the table play, is paramount.

♦ ♣ ♥ ♠

WHERE TO
PLAY POKER

CASINOS, ONLINE
AND OTHER
OPPORTUNITIES

Live Action

Poker is the most adaptable of games: a pack of cards and at least one other player is basically all you need. Popular as a parlour game from the mid-19th century, the home is still a good place to learn the rules and hone your skills before hitting the highlights of a casino or risking your luck online, while the impact of television poker has hugely increased play over the domestic table.

Despite the enormous growth of online poker sites, the allure of the casino is undeniable. Only here can you get the feel of the action, smell the sweat, and taste the atmosphere (usually tinged with tobacco). Remember, a lot of casinos will not maintain poker rooms, so check before you go if poker is your game of choice. A list of casinos in Russia alone, which mushroomed in the wake of *perestroika*, would fill the pages of this book and more, so our selection is necessarily very selective, and only includes the ones featuring poker rooms. A worldwide selection appears on page 232.

The Top Ten Poker Rooms

Although poker has become a global phenomenon, its heart and soul is still definitely rooted in the USA. That's why the majority of this list is comprised of American casinos, although we have managed to include some from other corners of the globe.

Bellagio Las Vegas, Nevada, USA

Made famous, or should we say more famous, by the recent *Ocean's 11* and *Ocean's 12* films, the Bellagio is pure glamour and glitz. It has a state-of the-art poker room that cost millions of dollars to build and is the obvious choice for first on this list. If you do happen to win big on any of the 30 tables, try not to blow it all in one of the many top-grade and very pricey restaurants in the complex.

♦ ♣ ♥ ♠

LAS VEGAS

The casinos in Las Vegas are widely distributed across the city area, but most of the main venues are clustered around the Strip and Downtown. Currently, Rio hosts the main WSOP events.

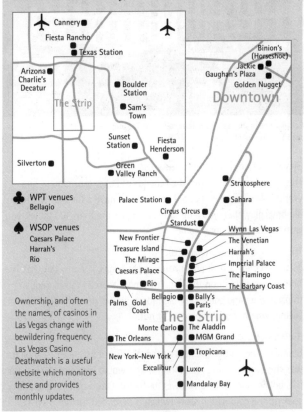

♣ WPT venues
Bellagio

♠ WSOP venues
Caesars Palace
Harrah's
Rio

Ownership, and often the names, of casinos in Las Vegas change with bewildering frequency. Las Vegas Casino Deathwatch is a useful website which monitors these and provides monthly updates.

Bellagio, one of the most glamorous casinos on The Strip, recently invested in an ultra-modern poker room.

Bicycle Casino Los Angeles, California, USA

This casino is host to both the Legends of Poker tournament and World Poker Tour events, so if you want to have a taste of where the big boys play, then you'll get it here. With more than 100 tables, you won't struggle to get a game.

The Mirage, Las Vegas, Nevada, USA

As the second-largest poker room in Las Vegas, it's only fair that The Mirage comes high on this list. With more than 24 tables, regular tournaments and some very big money action, it's definitely worth seeing, whether you're playing or not.

Binion's Las Vegas, Nevada, USA

Binion's is no longer the host of the WSOP, but as the Horseshoe it was the event's home for so long that it would be simply wrong for this poker room to be any lower in the list. Play a game there and soak up the colourful history (which is described further on p.41).

Aviation Club Paris, France

It might surprise some people to see a French poker room in the top five, but the Aviation Club is well worth its ranking. Stylish, classy and a kingpin venue on the European Poker Tour.

Commerce Casino Los Angeles, California, USA

It calls itself the poker capital of the world, and while we wouldn't go that far, it does warrant a high place on this top ten list. It has more than 125 poker tables and top tournaments such as the LA Poker Classic. What more could you ask?

Wynn Casino Las Vegas, Nevada, USA

This poker room, which was opened in spring 2005, cost nearly $3 million to put together, and has had rave reviews from the experts. It has 27 tables, is truly state of the art (automatic card shufflers, electronic sign-up system) and well worth a visit.

Taj Mahal Atlantic City, New Jersey, USA

If any of Atlantic City's poker rooms deserve to make this list, it's this one. It's widely regarded as the most popular poker room in New Jersey, has 68 tables and is host to the US Poker Championship.

Hollywood Park Casino Inglewood, California, USA

Any casino that is home to a school of poker deserves to make a top ten for that alone. On top of housing the Mike Caro University of Poker, Hollywood Park also hosts a number of major poker tournaments, along with daily ones for the regular punter.

The Grosvenor Victoria Casino London, UK

As one of the largest and oldest casino clubs in Britain, the Grosvenor Victoria sneaks on to the list. Found in the heart of London, it has a 100-seat card room and plenty of tournaments in which to make your mark.

Eyes on the Future

The spread and distribution of casinos is of course linked to often sticky local or national legislation. This explains why offshore havens (Aruba, Macao), liberal local city administrations (Reno, Las Vegas, Atlantic City, or Sun City in South Africa), enclaves (Monte Carlo, or opportunist non-Federal sites like Native American reservations in the US) have long been magnets for serious players, but also explains the patchy distribution of gaming establishments generally. Recent debates in the UK illustrate the problem: gambling remained the province of private 'gentleman's' clubs until three decades ago, when licensed premises opened. Even then there was a wait of 24 hours between registration and access to the floor. Recent proposals to open seven 'Super Casinos' in resorts such as Blackpool foundered on the reefs of parliamentary indecision.

However, the impact of the online gambling boom is having its effect in eroding the strength of the anti-gaming lobby. It has also seen the revival of Atlantic City, on its knees by the early 1980s, and the growth of centres such as Macao. In fact, with the liberalization of the Chinese economy, this tiny former Portuguese colony off southern China (population c.500,000) is experiencing a major boom. It enjoyed 47% growth in 2003-04, and is predicted to exceed Las Vegas' revenues in 2005. Although little poker is currently played here, the impact of televised and online poker in the US and Europe will soon be felt in Asia as well, especially as US casino brands such as Sands and Venetian are setting up in the 'Vegas of the East'.

Poker Cruises

The cruise industry is one of the biggest growth areas in tourism today. They happen all over the world – in the Mediterranean, the Caribbean, the Gulf of Mexico and even Alaska – and provide

♦ ♣ ♥ ♠

education and entertainment for the wealthy. Cruise ships have long offered the gambler the chance to play outside the territorial waters of countries where gaming is restricted. They are now becoming even more popular with the gaming fraternity. Never slow to spot an opportunity, the poker powers-that-be have jumped on the bandwagon and there are now a raft of big-money tournaments that take place on cruise ships, the majority of which are open to online qualifiers.

The Party Poker Million Cruise – which is televised and part of the World Poker Tour – sees more than 750 poker players battle it out for a prize pool in excess of $7 million. The 2005 winner, 24-year-old Michael Gracz, took home $1.5 million

Online Poker

One of the reasons for the success of online poker is that the leading sites offer a secure environment in which to play. It is simply not worth their while to rip off the punters – they make enough money from their typical 10% rake in cash games, and why would they risk bad publicity?

In sit-and-go tournament play, for instance, with a $30 buy-in, and a new table every five minutes, frequently over 1000 people can be playing at any one time. That's $36,000 earned by the host site every hour. Play money games which most online sites offer are effectively loss-leaders, designed to entice inexperienced players into the cash games once they have gained enough confidence.

The number of sites has grown hugely. But which one should you use? Ten of the biggest are listed below. All offer both real and play money options so the important differences lie in their graphics, reliability, ease to win money, and promotions.

www.partypoker.com

The largest poker site in the world, Party Poker frequently has more than twice as many players as its competitors, although this is achieved in part by people being fed through from other poker sites (you might actually log on to a different site, but still end up playing at Party Poker).

Plenty of high-value tournaments and good bonuses, coupled with no difficulties finding a game, mean Party Poker is an excellent site for everybody from a nervous beginner to a high-stakes rounder. Being the biggest, it has a huge marketing budget and so sponsors many tournaments and events, from Hollywood previews to cruises.

One of Party Poker's gaming rooms. ©PartyPoker.com

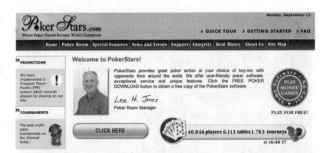

www.pokerstars.com

©PokerStars.com

Pokerstars are hosting the World Championship of Online Poker and therefore have many good players using their site. This makes it a bit daunting for beginners and novices, especially as there are no telephone support lines. However, it's easy to get a game, and the site did produce the WSOP main event winner in both 2003 (Chris Moneymaker) and 2004 (Greg Raymer).

www.pacificpoker.com

Loyalty bonuses for long-term players are good, but the graphics and software are less impressive than other sites. Excellent statistics history for players, so there is no excuse for not learning and improving. A superb site for loose play and easier than the others to win on.

www.gamingclub.com

An excellent sign-up bonus of up to $300 and many short-handed games make it easy to get a good table, although for the really big players there are fewer high-stakes options. For those who find one table is not enough, there is a four-table viewing option. There are also telephone support for problems and a detailed lobby with flop percentages and average pot information.

The Swedish-owned Pokerroom site offers sophisticated, virtually-real graphics and is easily accessible from most computer platforms. ©PartyRoom.com

www.pokerroom.com

One of the very few sites that needs no download. The software used works on Linux, Mac and more standard operating systems, although a download is available. The site is easy to navigate and there is a good signing-on bonus. Also frequent daily free-roll tournaments. Pokerroom recently launched poker games on mobile phones but, as yet, it is only for play money.

www.ultimatebet.com

Excellent software with a degree of personal choice for the background. Hosts its own event – the Aruba Classic – in the Caribbean, and is heavily endorsed by professionals like Phil Hellmuth Jnr. and Annie Duke. Good turbo events with added prizes guaranteed for those players who want a tournament to last less than a day or night, but sit-and-go tables are not popular.

©interpoker.com

www.interpoker.com
Euro, dollar or sterling currencies accepted, which is very useful and
rare – most sites are dollars only – leaving those not in the US to
pay currency charges. Many promotions and loose tables, but the
rake is quite expensive and the software unimpressive.

www.paradisepoker.com
Good graphics and traffic make it appealing, but the standard of
play is high, and signing and loyalty bonuses are poor. The ring
games are especially popular, as are tournaments and sit-and-go
tables. The rake is higher than other sites.

©ParadisePoker.com

©fulltiltpoker.com

www.fulltiltpoker.com

The site of Phil Ivey, Howard Lederer and Chris Ferguson amongst others. A superb signing bonus of up to $600. The professionals play on the site and attract players but this makes it less inviting for novices. The play money tables get good action, so it is a good site to learn the game without damaging the wallet.

www.williamhillpoker.com

Good monthly bonuses if you play more than 250 hands. As a European-based site there is the option of Euro, dollar or sterling currencies and the live telephone support is very useful. Importantly, this is one of the few European sites that can accept traffic from the US. However, the graphics are a bit tame and dull.

ONLINE CHEATING

Internet games might seem a reasonably safe arena for cheating, and a well-known scam is for two or three players to join an online game whilst comparing hands over the telephone. However, most sites have some form of artificial intelligence which monitors the games and individual playing patterns linked to the hands dealt. They also employ statisticians to analyze these patterns, and have the results independently audited. So don't be tempted.

♦ ♣ ♥ ♠

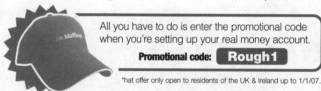

THE TOP
TOURNAMENTS

World Series of Poker (WSOP)

When Joseph Hachem turned his cards over to reveal he had a straight 3 to 7, the world had a new poker champion. It was nearly 7am on Saturday July 16, 2005. The final table of the WSOP's No-Limit Texas Hold'em championship event had been running some 15 hours, and at last the remaining two players were all-in. Hachem, whose opponent had a Pair of Aces, had won, becoming the 36th WSOP title winner, scooping $7.5 million.

How times have changed. When Johnny Moss won the 1971 title – which he had retained from the previous year – he received $30,000. A not inconsiderable sum, but it pales into insignificance when compared to subsequent first place prizes. By 1980 the top prize passed $300,000, in 1989 it was more than $750,000 and by 1991 it reached the magic $1 million mark. That's healthy inflation, but in the following years things really went nuts. In 2000, the winner took home $1.5 million – and the 2005 WSOP champion won five times that amount. So big have the first prizes become in recent years that the winner of each has shot straight in at number one in the all-time money winners' list. Future winners will undoubtedly do the same.

Demand to play in the event has never been higher and as it increases each year, so does the number of participants. In 2005 there were 5,619 players vying for the championship title – that's more than double the 2,576 who competed in the previous year's championship event. With each of these seats in the tournament costing $10,000 (some are paid for directly by the players, others by the websites who run the online satellite qualifying tournaments), it's easy to understand why the prize money just keeps on growing.

♦ ♣ ♥ ♠

WSOP ALL-TIME MONEY WINNERS LIST

Name	Prize	WSOP Champion	Money finishes	WSOP Bracelets
Joe Hachem	$7,525,850	2005	2	1
Greg Raymer	$5,433,450	2004	5	1
Steven Dannenmann	$4,250,000	0	1	0
Johnny Chan	$3,744,331	1987,1988	29	10
T. J. Cloutier	$3,697,251	0	43	6
David Williams	$3,507,705	0	2	0
Dan Harrington	$3,472,858	1995	8	2
Phil Hellmuth Jr.	$3,406,705	1989	42	9
Josh Arieh	$3,188,590	0	8	2
Chris Ferguson	$3,121,456	2000	42	5
Erik Seidel	$3,039,748	0	36	7
Chris Moneymaker	$2,521,000	2003	2	1
Tex Barch	$2,500,000	0	1	0
Doyle Brunson	$2,232,019	1976, 1977	24	10
Stu Ungar	$2,068,650	1980, 1981, 1997	13	5
Dewey Tomko	$2,013,593	0	28	3
Aaron Kanter	$2,000,000	0	1	0
Robert Varkonyi	$2,000,000	2002	1	1
Scotty Nguyen	$1,975,922	1998	28	4
Mike Matusow	$1,953,190	0	15	2

It's all such a long way from 1969 when a handful of top poker players were invited to the Riverside Casino in Reno, Nevada, by its owner, Tom Morehead, to take part in what is regarded as the first World Series of Poker. It wasn't called as such – its name was The Texas Gamblers' Reunion – and wasn't really a tournament either, as there was no winner at the end. Everyone who took part just played poker for one week solid and then went home. Nevertheless, the event attracted a healthy amount of public interest and all the big names in gambling. Doyle Brunson, Amarillo Slim, Johnny Moss, and even Charles Harrelson (father of actor Woody) were there. So was the legendary Benny Binion, owner of Las Vegas's Horseshoe casino, who saw the potential to turn the event into something massive.

Binion was a master at public relations and had seen how high-stakes poker can excite the public when in 1949 he'd organized a five-month long marathon match between the two most highly-regarded gamblers of the time, Johnny Moss and Nick 'the Greek' Dandalos. During that epic match – which is reported to have cost Dandalos at least as much as $2 million – huge crowds had gathered at the Horseshoe casino to catch a glimpse of the action. Twenty years later, Binion put two and two together and the idea for an annual tournament was born. When Morehead sold his casino shortly after The Texas Gamblers' Reunion, Binion acquired the rights to his tournament and set about organizing the first event to actually be called the World Series of Poker, to be held in the early summer of 1970.

He opened a poker room in the Horseshoe, filled it with America's greatest gamblers and hosted high-profile poker-fest. All the top players were there. They just turned up and played poker for a while and that was enough for Binion to christen the gathering the World

♦ ♣ ♥ ♠

Series. But it still wasn't a tournament in the sense that we know it today. When the players had had enough, they voted for who they thought had been the best. On that basis, Johnny Moss became the first poker world champion. There was no structure, though, and for this reason the event didn't attract the hoped-for publicity. As one American journalist pointed out, it was like asking people to watch a Kentucky Derby in which the jockeys rode round and round a track with no finish line and then decided who had won by mutual consent. Where was the excitement in that? The WSOP had to be pepped up before Binion's grand vision could be realized.

In 1971, the first knockout WSOP was staged. Six players paid $5,000 each to enter a match in which only one of them would walk away with the entire $30,000. Johnny Moss eliminated the opposition to became world champion for the second time (though in many people's eyes this was the first time he'd managed it for real). This new tournament style of play, christened freeze-out, began attracting more interest and the WSOP started to grow, although modestly at first. By 1972, eight players were competing in a $10,000 buy-in, winner-takes-all event, and poker legend Amarillo Slim scooped the $80,000 prize. All this is still quite small by today's standards, but the most important part of the 1972 tournament was not the number of players or the money involved, but the media attention it generated. Although live coverage and under-the-table cameras were still a long way off, television bosses became interested in the personalities involved in the game. In the wake of Slim's 1972 victory, both he and Binion appeared on a host of prime-time programmes including Johnny Carson's *Tonight Show* and *60 Minutes*. Binion and Slim were soon both household names. The WSOP had come of age and it has since gone from strength to strength.

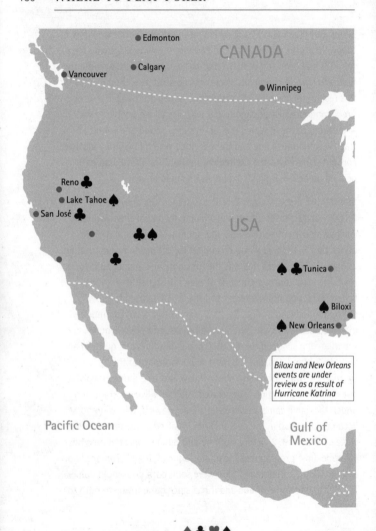

Edmonton

CANADA

Calgary

Vancouver

Winnipeg

Reno ♣

Lake Tahoe ♠

San José ♣

USA

♣ ♠

♣

♠ ♣ Tunica

♠ Biloxi

♠ New Orleans

Biloxi and New Orleans events are under review as a result of Hurricane Katrina

Pacific Ocean

Gulf of Mexico

♦ ♣ ♥ ♠

Major casinos

World Poker Tour

World Series of Poker Tour

Quebec

Mashantucket

Atlantic City

Elizabeth

Atlantic Ocean

BAHAMAS
Paradise Island (Nassau)

DOMINICAN
REPUBLIC

Sint Maarten

Santa Domingo

Antigua

Martinique

Caribbean Sea

Aruba
Curaçao

THE WSOP CHAMPIONS

Year	Winner	Nationality	Money won
2005	Joseph Hachem	Australia	$7.5million
2004	Greg Raymer	USA	$5million
2003	Chris Moneymaker	USA	$2.5million
2002	Robert Varkonyi	USA	$2million
2001	Carlos Mortensen	Spain	$1.5milion
2000	Chris Ferguson	USA	$1.5million
1999	JJ 'Noel' Furlong	Ireland	$1million
1998	Scotty Nguyen	USA	$1million
1997	Stu Ungar	USA	$1million
1996	Huck Seed	USA	$1million
1995	Dan Harrington	USA	$1million
1994	Russ Hamilton	USA	$1million
1993	Jim Bechtel	USA	$1million
1992	Hamid Dastmalchi	USA	$1million
1991	Brad Daugherty	USA	$1million
1990	Mansour Matloubi	Wales	$895,000
1989	Phil Hellmuth	USA	$755,000
1988	Johnny Chan	USA	$700,000

More interest meant more players wanting to take part and the demand for more poker variants to be included. So, in 1973, a Five-Card Stud competition was added to the headline No-Limit Texas Hold'em event. The number of separate tournaments within the WSOP has proliferated in subsequent years, reaching a peak in 2005 of 42. Many of the main poker games are now included, each offering a healthy cash sum, a coveted WSOP bracelet and a place in history to the winners. These days you can play limit Hold'em, pot

♦ ♣ ♥ ♠

Year	Winner	Nationality	Money won
1987	Johnny Chan	USA	$625,000
1986	Berry Johnston	USA	$570,000
1985	Bill Smith	USA	$700,000
1984	Jack Keller	USA	$660,000
1983	Tom McEvoy	USA	$580,000
1982	Jack Straus	USA	$520,000
1981	Stu Ungar	USA	$375,000
1980	Stu Ungar	USA	$385,000
1979	Hal Fowler	USA	$270,000
1978	Bobby Baldwin	USA	$210,000
1977	Doyle Brunson	USA	$340,000
1976	Doyle Brunson	USA	$220,000
1975	Sailor Roberts	USA	$210,000
1974	Johnny Moss	USA	$160,000
1973	Puggy Pearson	USA	$130,000
1972	Amarillo Slim	USA	$80,000
1971	Johnny Moss	USA	$30,000
1970	Johnny Moss	USA	NA

limit Hold'em, pot limit Omaha, Omaha High/Low split, Seven-Card Stud, Razz and many others, all with buy-ins ranging from $500 to $10,000. There are even seniors-only, women-only and casino employee-only tournaments on offer.

The WSOP's breadth and depth is now simply enormous and would doubtless make its creator and architect Benny Binion, who died on Christmas Day 1989, a very proud man. Even he could not have dreamed of it growing into the behemoth it has become, although he knew he was on to something very special even in the early days. 'This poker game here gets us a lot of attention,' Binion is reported to have said after the 1973 WSOP. 'We had eight players last year, and this year we had 13. I look to have better than 20 next year. It's even liable to get up to be 50, might get up to be more than that.' Binion then paused, 'It will eventually.'

It has, and with online and televised poker feeding more and more people into the game, the exponential growth won't slow down. In 2005 more than 23,000 people took part in the 42 WSOP events, playing for a total prize pool of more than $100 million. Big crowds now come to watch the event live, ESPN and other major networks broadcast the event worldwide, and there's substantial coverage in the global press too. Small wonder, considering the number of terrific stories that the WSOP has thrown up over the years.

In 1982, for instance, Jack Straus came back from a poker grave after losing a hand he thought he had gone all-in on. When the hand was over he was all set to leave the table when he found a single $500 chip. From that point on he never looked back and eventually completed an astounding victory on the final table.

Then in 1997, two-times winner Stu Ungar, who had had a well-documented drug problem for decades, couldn't afford the buy-in fee. So his friend, six-time WSOP bracelet winner Billy Baxter, gave him the money. Ungar went on to win the $1 million first prize. And now, celebrities are getting in on the act with a well-known actress winning the ladies event in 2005. As many have been eager to point out since, she may never win an Oscar, but Jennifer Tilly will always be the first Hollywood star to win a WSOP bracelet.

♦ ♣ ♥ ♠

WSOP Today

The rights to the tournament have belonged to the huge entertainment corporation, Harrah's – who own numerous casinos around the world, including the Rio in Las Vegas – since they purchased Binion's Horseshoe casino in 2004. They renamed the casino Binion's and subsequently sold it. The final table of the 2005 championship event was held there in 2005, but the vast majority of WSOP tournaments were held at the Rio and that's where all of the 2006 tournament events will take place.

The WSOP brand is being brought in to the 21st century and Harrah's will be expanding it massively throughout 2006 in an attempt to mimic the success of the World Poker Tour. A WSOP tour

Actress and poker ace Jennifer Tilley at the London Open in summer 2005, fresh from her success in the ladies event at the WSOP.

was held in August 2005, and included 12 events in a number of US cities such as Las Vegas, Atlantic City, Lake Tahoe and Tunica. Planned events in Biloxi and New Orleans were cancelled at the last minute following the devastation of Hurricane Katrina. The winners of each of the $10,000 buy-in No-Limit Texas Hold'em events will qualify for the WSOP Tournament of Champions that will take place in late June 2006 just before the World Series of Poker itself begins. Twenty-seven players – comprising the 12 circuit tournament winners, the nine players from the 2005–06 World Series of Poker final table, and six players chosen by the tournament's sponsors – will compete for a $2 million prize pool.

Almost anyone can win the World Series of Poker championship event these days, and you don't even have to have $10,000 for the buy-in fee. With all the big online poker rooms offering satellite tournaments, becoming world champion is a dream any amateur can now realize. If you don't believe it, remember that around 1000 of the championship players in 2004 won their seats online and that both the 2003 and 2004 winners – Chris Moneymaker and Greg Raymer respectively – qualified through Pokerstars.com. In fact Moneymaker, an accountant who'd never played in a live in-the-flesh game before the 2003 WSOP – paid only $40 for the privilege.

The World Poker Tour (WPT)

The World Poker Tour, or WPT as it is more commonly known, was the brainchild of a television executive called Steve Lipscomb and a Hall of Famer turned business executive, Lyle Berman. Lipscomb was sent in the late 1990s to film a feature on the WSOP, and he realized that with 50 million poker players in the US and probably double that (at least) worldwide, there was potential for a weekly televised poker show. The problem was how to translate the tension and excitement of big-money poker games to the screen. The answer was under-the-table cameras showing the television audience exactly what hole cards each player has. All that was needed after that was a prize fund large enough to run a small country; the natural greed of mankind and the glamour of instant (and huge) wealth would provide the rest. And they were right. Now in Season Four, the WPT, originally commissioned by the *Travel Channel* in the US in 2003, is a worldwide television show broadcast on over 100 channels with many spin-off shows, like the celebrity events or tournaments of champions. It has been so successful that, since airing online, the number of players has increased more than five-fold, and the show itself has become the highest-rated ever shown on the *Travel Channel*.

One of the main reasons for this success is its high production values which separate the WPT from other televised poker shows. In addition, not only are the locations and final table viewer-friendly, but the table chat is clearly audible and often humorous, the audience is enthralled with the action that is taking place yards from them, and the commentators and hosts excellent: Mike Sexton, himself a world-famous poker player, lends each programme a certain gravitas and authority, while his more excitable sidekick, Vince van Patten, a former tennis professional on the ATP tour (with a highest ranking of 26), a former child actor, scriptwriter and scourge of home games in Hollywood, injects more humour for the novice viewers. Providing the female glamour is Shana Hiatt, a former model turned actress and host of E! Entertainment's *Wild Show*. She offers links and segues, and quizzes those just eliminated. Admittedly these may not be the most searching of journalistic enquiries, but the show is about the tension and the money, and that is what it concentrates on.

In Season Four in 2005/06 the WPT consisted of 16 events, mostly in America, but with the Caribbean and France also featured. If Doyle Brunson has his way, it may well change again, as in 2005 he launched a $700 million cash bid for the WPT.

The European Poker Tour (EPT)

The vision of a former Ladbrokes Poker Million winner, television executive Jon Duthie, the European Poker Tour brings televised high-stakes poker tournaments to venues across Europe, courtesy of Pokerstars.com. In its first season, in 2004, the EPT visited six different European countries, culminating in a glamorous finale in exclusive Monte Carlo. The prize pool in the final event was in excess of 2 million euros, making it the largest poker tournament held in Europe. Sponsored exclusively by www.pokerstars.com, the EPT expanded to include an event in Baden, Austria for Season Two to go with the events in Barcelona, Dublin, London, Copenhagen, Deauville and the finale in Monte Carlo. One regular on the EPT is former US Open Tennis champion, Yevgeny Kafelnikov, although the Grand Final winner of Season One was a middle-aged Dutchman, caring family man and long-time gambler, Rob Hollink.

World Poker Exchange

A new event which grabbed headlines in 2005 was the London Open, hosted by World Poker Exchange, which claims to be the first major live tournament mounted by a online poker business. With a $2 million prize at stake, this high profile pro-celeb tournament saw poker stars such as Doyle Brunson, Gus Hansen, Mimi Rogers, and cross-over celebrity Jennifer Tilley at table with UK horseracing pundit John McCririck and a host of young aspirants. The event was won by Iwan Jones who walked away with $750,000.

♦ ♣ ♥ ♠

POKER
CULTURE

POKER CULTURE

A Game for the Masses

Poker entered our cultural history at an interesting time. The early 19th century witnessed many changes: the beginnings of modern republicanism; mass migration, not just to the New World of the Americas, but also through the colonies of the Old World; and the rise of an entrepreneurial middle class alongside the emergence of a powerful industrial working class. Both had their own ways of passing time – usually involving the possibility of enrichment. Card games, hitherto conducted in bars and brothels, became acceptable among the middle and upper classes, while the possibility of cleaning up at the table, and thus raising one's social stakes from poverty to wealth, attracted many further down the social ladder. Poker dovetailed almost perfectly with the American Dream of advancement and enrichment. From the early 19th century, gambling, and specifically poker, gained an iconic importance in many artistic pursuits, from opera and the stage, to literature and – in the 20th century – the cinema.

Poker and Philosophy

Poker as we know it was probably not played before the 19th century, but it is clear that the French mathematician and natural philosopher Blaise Pascal (1623-62) was fascinated by the numerical possibilities and potential outplay of the pack of cards. His theory of probability describes a mathematical function much admired by the more numerically-minded poker players, and the principles of odds were explored further by Fermat (1601-65). Cards appear in another mathematician's work, the 19th-century Oxford scholar Charles Dodgson who, as Lewis Carroll, included The Queen of Hearts and her court in *Alice in Wonderland* (1865).

♦ ♣ ♥ ♠

Poker on the Page

The great Russian Romantic and Realist novelists of the 19th century were among the first writers to treat vying games as central themes in their work. The fact that the expanding Russian empire had varied contacts with neighbouring cultures – Persians, Chinese, and Americans in Alaska – probably contributed to this. While Russian

Alice encounters the Queen of Hearts in Wonderland from Lewis Carroll's classic.

Roulette remains the most notorious gambling game of all, it also reflects the love of games of chance and skill which lie near the heart of the Russian psyche.

Widely regarded as the father of modern Russian literature, Alexander Pushkin, if not a card-player himself, was aware of the allure of the green baize. His tales of military life on the eastern frontiers frequently feature officers whiling away their time on cardplay. His story *The Queen Of Hearts* tells of an ambitious young man obsessed with finding the winning formula at cards. Fyodor Dostoyevsky went on to write *The Gambler*, which uses the fatal obsession with chance as its central theme. Both of Tolstoy's masterpieces, *War and Peace* (1869) and *Anna Karenina* (1877), feature vying cardplay – usually as a metaphor for decadence and a reliance by the characters on chance to determine their destiny.

But it was the poets, observers and satirists of the American frontier who first seized upon the unique dynamics and language of poker

♦ ♣ ♥ ♠

as a source of imagery and tension in their tale-telling. Mark Twain (1835-1910), is outstanding here (see page 168), but poker games feature also in the tales of Jack London and the work of 'Poets of the Rushes', Bret Harte and Robert Service.

> *"There are few things so unpardonably neglected in our country as poker...It is enough to make you blush".*
>
> MARK TWAIN

Literary links to the green baize continued in a somewhat different vein in the interwar years, as writers such as Damon Runyon and Dashiell Hammett began to explore and glamourise the American 'low-life' cultures in which they set their tales. Meanwhile, on the high table, literary giants such as William Faulkner were doing the same thing. Today, leading writers like Alvarez, Saul Bellow, John Updike and Norman Mailer have tackled poker head-on, while crime novelists such as Elmore Leonard and Carl Hiassen feature crackling poker scenes in their crime novels.

Top Ten Writings on Poker

Today, it is difficult to find a literary 'name' who isn't an avowed poker fan, either player, railguard, or one who has not used the narrative or dynamics of poker to dramatic effect at some point in their work.

Al Alvarez *The Biggest Game in Town* Houghton Mifflin, 1983
Al Alvarez might seem an unlikely candidate to write one of the definitive works on poker. Born in London in 1929, Alvarez championed the work of poets like John Berryman, Ted Hughes and

♦ ♣ ♥ ♠

Sylvia Plath as a literary critic in the
1960s. But Alvarez is also a regular
player and an insightful observer of
the game. *The Biggest Game in Town*
(originally a series of articles in *The
New Yorker* magazine), chronicled the
1981 WSOP, and was hailed by the *San
Francisco Chronicle* as a 'magnificent
book' and by London's *Evening
Standard* as 'probably the best book on
poker ever written'. It remains a must-
read for anyone who plays poker at any

Al Alvarez, doyen of serious
poker writers outside his home.

level. More recently, Alvarez authored another study of the game,
Poker: Bets, Bluffs, and Bad Beats (Chronicle, 2001).

Andy Bellin *Poker Nation* Harper Collins, 2002
Subtitled 'A high-stakes, low-life adventure into the heart of a
gambling country' and described by its publisher as "part memoir,
part exposé, and part how-to (or how not-to)", *Poker Nation* is the
highly entertaining story of how Bellin – a graduate student in
astrophysics – dropped out of academia and into the gritty world of
underground, 'semipro' poker, for more than a decade.

Anthony Holden *Big Deal: One Year as a Professional Poker Player*
TransWorld Publishers Ltd, 1990
Lancashire-born Holden made his literary name in the 1980s with
biographies of the British royal family, Shakespeare and Tchaikovsky,
but in 1990, Holden decided to spend a year as a pro player (he
finished some $12,000 up). Out of this experience came *Big Deal*,
which Holden describes as the only one of his books that 'was as
much fun to write as to research'.

Mark Twain, wit, raconteur and an early advocate of poker.

Mark Twain *'The Professor's Yarn'* from *Life on the Mississippi* 1883
Author of the classics *Huckleberry Finn* and *Tom Sawyer*, Mark Twain (the pen name of Samuel Clemens) became acquainted with poker as a steamboat pilot on the Mississippi during the golden age of riverboat gambling, and remained an avid player for the rest of his life. *The Professor's Yarn* is one of the earliest poker-centred stories, a variation on a theme that runs through the literature of gambling – the supposed 'sucker' who turns the tables on the cardsharps.

David Mamet *'Things I Learned Playing Poker on the Hill'* from *Writing in Restaurants* Viking, 1986
One of the most acclaimed American dramatists of recent decades, Mamet has also written and directed films including *House of Games* (1987, see page 182) . Gamblers and conmen inhabit many of Mamet's works, which are renowned for their terse, hard-boiled dialogue. This essay distils Mamet's observations from two decades of play in a regular 'friendly game.'

James McManus *Positively Fifth Street* Farrar, Straus and Giroux, 2003
Like Alvarez, McManus is a poet and novelist with a sideline in poker. In 2000, *Harper's* magazine commissioned him to cover that year's WSOP. McManus put up his fee as a stake, entered the tournament

♦ ♣ ♥ ♠

himself, and walked away from the final table as the fifth-place winner, $250,000 richer. McManus's account of his astonishing performance is interweaved with the story of the Binion murder case (see pages 40–43). McManus now teaches what is perhaps the only college course in poker literature, at The School of the Art Institute of Chicago.

Paul Auster *The Music of Chance* Viking, 1990
The Music of Chance centres on Nashe, an ex-fireman drifting across the country living off a dwindling inheritance, and Pozzi, the professional gambler who 'befriends' him. Pozzi convinces Nashe to use his remaining money to bankroll a poker game with a pair of rich, eccentric recluses. What was supposed to be an easy score goes awry, and Nashe and Pozzi are set a very unusual task to pay off their debt. A highly existential work that some critics have compared to Beckett's *Waiting for Godot*, it was filmed in 1999.

Patrick Marber *Dealer's Choice* 1995
British writer, actor, and comedian Marber drew on his own experience as a compulsive gambler (he has said that at his worst, he lost as much as £10,000 a night – money he didn't have) for this drama, in which a waiter with a gambling problem, Sweeney, is drawn into a game with the owner of the restaurant in which he works. The taut table dialogue is as good as it gets.

Jesse May *Shut Up and Deal* Anchor Books, 1998
'There is no reality away from the poker table', proclaims Mickey, the protagonist of this rambling (and presumably autobiographical) novel. Set mostly in American casino poker rooms in the 1990s, the book is populated by the people who both play to live and live to play, and May brilliantly captures the ups and downs of their lives.

He went on to become a commentator on Late Night Poker, the pioneering poker show on Britain's Channel Four.

John Updike *'Poker Night'* from *Trust Me* Knopf, 1987
Originally published in *Esquire* magazine, this short story from one of America's greatest postwar fiction writers is written in the voice of a small-town businessman who faithfully attends his weekly poker game, despite having received some very bad news beforehand.

Poker in Song
The fact that poker was widely regarded, by the mid-19th century, not only as the 'cheating game', but also claimed as a national institution by the young US republic, has provided endless possibilities to song-writers.

Both Blues music and its country cousin, Bluegrass, are riddled with poetic references to poker in all its forms. As so often, many of

THE GRATEFUL DEAD

Having been the house band at Ken Kesey's 'Acid Tests', and provided the soundtrack to the Summer of Love, the Grateful Dead reinvented themselves as narrators and archivists of American folklore in the classic albums **American Beauty** and **Workingman's Dead**. The songs on these two albums, the classic live albums of the period,

The Death's Head Joker, one of many of the Dead's images created by Kelly/Mouse.

these songs seem to draw on a common folk or cultural memory, as if poker, like love and fate, is a central aspect of life, and needs no explanation beyond the song itself. It is in this form that poker imagery has sifted down into Country and Western songwriting, as a lens through which the human condition may be analyzed, the game as metaphor for life and the way it might be lived. 'Me And My Uncle', a rather uncharacteristic song by John Philips, first recorded by the ubiquitous Judy Collins, is an exemplar of this process. A dark cowboy tale, the song narrates the travels of a young rounder with his uncle, a steamy poker game which ends in blood, the uncle grabbing the pot, and a shocking twist when the rounder turns on his uncle, guns him down and makes off with the winnings. As the narrator claims, ruefully, his uncle 'taught me good. Lord, taught me all I know'.

Not surprising then that Bob Dylan picked up on the imagery of

and lead guitarist/visionary Jerry Garcia's first solo album, largely comprise the work of the band's chief lyricist, Robert Hunter, whose verse is redolent of the American West, and whose imagery draws on the myths and images of poker. Songs such as 'Deal' and 'Loser' examine the gambler's dilemma, including memorable lines such as: 'If I had a gun for every Ace I have drawn, I could arm a town the size of Abilene', and 'Don't you push me baby, 'cos I'm on an Inside Straight, and you know I'm only in it for the gold'. Most enigmatic is his description of a seemingly impossibly high hand, in 'Ramblin' Rose': 'Sittin' plush with a Royal Flush, Aces back-to-back', a situation only possible with an Ace 'cuter' on the board.

10 BEST POKER SONGS

The Stranger Song	Leonard Cohen
Turn the Cards Slowly	Patsy Cline
The Name of the Game is Stud	Tom Paxton
The Gambler	Kenny Rogers
Poker	Electric Light Orchestra
Five Card Stud	Ace Frehley
The Moonlight Gambler	Frankie Laine
Loser	Grateful Dead
Me and My Uncle	Judy Collins
The Queen of Draw Poker Town	Hank Snow

cards, especially in his adaptations of traditional songs such as 'Down the Highway' (1963) – 'Well I been gamblin' so long, Lord I ain't got much more to lose' – and 'Delia' (1993). However, he doesn't use it as much as one would expect. In an early interview on the radio programme *Folksinger's Choice* (1960) he claims he couldn't 'read' cards. But gamblers feature regularly in his carnival of characters, from John Wesley Hardin(g) to Frankie Lee – 'the Gambler, whose father is deceased'.

'Tell me what you're gonna do, when the Devil calls your cards' Dylan asks in 'Whatcha Gonna Do' (1963), while 'Lily, Rosemary and the Jack of Hearts' (1974) is a gambling novella in its own right, – 'Backstage the girls were playin' Five Card Stud by the stairs, Lily had two Queens for a third to match her pair' – and throughout the song's 16 verses, card characters recur. The Queen of Spades makes an appearance as the name of a bar in 'I Want You' (1966).

♦ ♣ ♥ ♠

North of the 49th parallel, poet/songwriter Leonard Cohen penned one of the finest poker songs ever – 'The Stranger Song'. The rock era has seen several other poker- or card-based allusions, from songs like the recurrent versions of 'Jack o' Diamonds' to Motorhead's 'Ace of Spades', and album covers like Bob Weir's *Ace* and the J. Geils Band's *Full House*.

Poker on Stage and Screen

Not the most obvious of choices for tense drama, especially on stage where the audience cannot actually see what is happening at the table, poker nevertheless features as an important structural aspect of several plays and operas. *The Beggar's Opera* and *La Traviata* feature cardplay, and Tennessee Williams' *A Streetcar Named Desire* had its origins in a one-act piece called *The Poker Night*.

Critical poker scenes however have long featured as part of the staple fare of that most American of cinematic fantasies

Vivien Leigh trying to lure Marlon Brando from the table in *A Streetcar Named Desire* (Kazan, 1951)

– the Western. Indeed, many Westerns use poker as a central theme, including *5-Card Stud* (Hathaway, 1968) featuring Dean Martin as a sharp, and the under-used poker face of Robert Mitchum. Few genuine characters from the old West have escaped apotheosis as poker masters (or mistresses) on the silver screen in movies like *Dodge City* (Curtiz, 1939), *My Darling Clementine* (Ford, 1946) and *Tombstone* (Cosmatis,

♦ ♣ ♥ ♠

1993). Facility at the table (and the ability to detect a cheat and serve him his just desserts down the barrel of a gun) remains a basic attribute of the Western hero. It is no accident that the long-running television series *Maverick* (1957-61), featuring the charm and guile of James Garner (not someone you would want to play poker against), ran for 138 episodes, and was revived in 1994 as a feature film starring Mel Gibson in Garner's role.

On television, from the mid-1950s whole episodes of *Bonanza*, *Wagon Train*, *Have Gun Will Travel*, *Rawhide*, *Laramie*, *The Westerner*, *The Iron Horse*, *The Virginian*, *Rifleman*, and *Branded* focused on the poker table, while latter-day TV oaters like *The High Chaparral* and *Alias Smith and Jones* often used poker scenarios as 'moral' lessons for their heroes. Undoubtedly, the prince of screen poker sharks was Brian Donleavy, clipped moustache , shifty-eyed and unscrupulous, but the mere appearance of a sweaty-lipped Warren Oates, snake-eyed Harry Dean Stanton or desperate and unshaven natural losers like Elisha J Cook or Strother Martin would normally signal a scene at the table.

On the other side of the Atlantic, one of the few TV shows to focus on poker (and the gambling life in general) was *Big Deal* (1984-86), featuring world-weary Ray Brooks as Robbie Box, scheming and scamming the smoky backroom gaming parlours of West London.

The very portability of poker – it only requires a pack of cards and players who 'are willing' – has also contributed to its enduring popularity. Tales are legion of film crews led by John Ford, Howard Hawks, Raoul Walsh or John Huston loitering, on desolate locations such as Monument Valley, over card tables; of roadies biding their time with some hands between rock group 'load ins' and 'load outs'.

Pat Garrett and Billy the Kid

Although arguable that this major post-modern Western movie is one of the great poker movies, it has a lot going for it. The director, Sam Peckinpah, flush from the success of *The Wild Bunch* (1969, no poker) and the notoriety of *Straw Dogs* (1971, again no poker) was nevertheless a keen poker player off-set. He had been slated to direct *The Cincinnati Kid* in 1965 but, as elsewhere in his career, had screwed up at the last minute. Brought up on a ranch, and steeped in Western culture (his grandmother was a Paiute Indian) Peckinpah was aware of the importance of poker as an intrinsic aspect of Western life and myth. His first feature film, *The Deadly Companions* (1961) opens with the central character entering a saloon to find his long-time quarry (an ex-adversary from the Civil War) bound and hanging from the ceiling while a poker game is in hand. He's hanging there because he cheated.

When Peckinpah got around to filming *Pat Garrett and Billy the Kid* (1973), he assembled an extraordinary range of talent. A grizzled James Coburn (also a poker player) came on board to play Garrett, while country singer-songwriter Kris Kristofferson took on the part of Billy. The script was by the underrated and under-employed Rudy Wurlitzer, who also appears (and is shot to pieces) in an opening cameo, while veterans like Jack Elam, Harry Dean Stanton, Paul Mix, Chill Wills, Katy Jurado and Slim Pickens take up various roles through the movie.

One of the many keys to the film is Bob Dylan (whose music Peckinpah claimed he had never heard beforehand), who not only provided an outstanding musical score (including his hit 'Knockin' on Heaven's Door' – radically cut from the revised Director's Cut version) but also plays the enigmatic Alias (the Joker?).

Near the beginning, the Kid is playing poker with his captors (reminiscent of the dice-playing centurions at the foot of the Cross) for his post-hanging chattels. As it happens, the Kid uses the *ennui* of low-action poker to effect his escape, notwithstanding the violent bluffing of one of his puritanical jailguards.

> *"Campin'out all night on the verandah*
> *Dealin' cards 'til dawn in the hacienda"*

BOB DYLAN, BILLY, 1972

Not just legend, but truth, has it that off-set in Mexico the long desert nights at Durango stretched to endless hands of poker washed down with tequila. Dylan builds considerable quantities of

Kris Kristofferson's Billy (left) plays for time with his captor Pat Garrett, played by a laconic James Coburn. The gun-toting religious zealot is played by R. G. Armstrong.

♦ ♣ ♥ ♠

poker-playing imagery into his songs, and the entire film can be read like a poker game, as the old friends Garrett and the Kid play bluff and double-bluff with each other, constantly raising the stakes. The pot, of course, turns out to be a bitter victory, with Garrett riding off into a dim dawn and squalid death, shot on the side of a road, having gunned down his best friend for money.

The 10 Best Poker Movies
Poker features in many movies, the best of which are listed below but, on the whole, it has to be said that cinema loves the characters who play the game more than the game itself. Some may complain that *A Big Hand for the Little Lady* (Cook, 1966) isn't included, but despite its focus on the game, it frankly isn't very good. And *The Music of Chance* (Haas, 1993) has already made it into the 10 Best Books (see page 169).

The Cincinnatti Kid Norman Jewison, 1965
Probably the first film to focus solely on poker and the personalities that inhabit its world, the film fits alongside *The Lusty Men* (Ray, 1952, rodeo), *Somebody Up There Likes Me* (Wise, 1958, boxing) and *The Hustler* (Rossen, 1961, pool), as a study of the psychology of the sportsman, the individual who chooses to put himself under pressure. Steve McQueen is the young tyro, Eric Stoner, who challenges the old pro Lancey Howard, played by Hollywood veteran Edward G. Robinson. Howard is the best, and Stoner manages to make his way into a high-stakes match against him. In the final scene Stoner is defeated, most improbably, by Howard. Critics, however, complain that if Stoner was as good as the rest of the film suggested, he would never have played his ultimate hand, but the film still portrays the tension of a high-stakes head-to-head battle to showdown. (See pages 162–163).

The Sting George Roy Hill, 1973

A follow-up vehicle for Paul Newman and Robert Redford in the wake of *Butch Cassidy and the Sundance Kid*, this film also dwells on period detail, but happily escapes the fate of having a 'Raindrops Keep Falling On My Head' sequence. In fact, Marvin Hamlisch's arrangements of Scott Joplin's music created a major revival of interest in ragtime and jazz. Set in Chicago in 1936, Robert Shaw is Donnie Lonnegan, a tough, no-nonsense man who cheats at the poker game he arranges on his usual train journey. Redford and Newman are conmen who target Lonnegan. Paul Newman plays a drunk, loud fool who irritates Lonnegan with his behaviour at the table. When Lonnegan and his henchman mark Newman with a new deck, Newman cheats and wins the pot.

> *"I know I gave him four Threes. He had to make a switch. We can't let him get away with that."*
> **"What was I supposed to do — call him for cheating better than me, in front of the others?"**

DAVID S WARD, THE STING, 1973

Bob le Flambeur Jean-Pierre Melville, 1956

Crafted by Melville, the Godfather of post-war French cinema and a leading player in the *nouvelle vague*, this film gets closer to the heart of gambling's allure than any other. Bob (Roger Duchesne) is a compulsive gambler but with honourable inclinations, shown by his help for a young prostitute that he takes under his wing. As his bankroll increases and decreases with every trip to the racetrack or casino, Bob hatches a plan to rob a casino of its safe. This is one of the seminal works of modern cinema, a French *film noir*, recently

♦ ♣ ♥ ♠

remade as *The Good Thief* (Jordan, 2001) with the swaggering Nick Nolte in the title role.

Kaleidoscope Jack Smight, 1966

Set in Swinging London, playboy gambler Warren Beatty breaks into a card manufacturer's and doctors the back of the printing plates so he can know what each card is when playing. Blackjack and poker wins follow, until the denouement when an arch-criminal challenges him and he has to play for his life – but with a different make of card. Susannah York and Jane Birkin wear some interesting clothes.

Rounders John Dahl, 1998

Spanning the gamut of poker scenarios from illicit backrooms to glitzy casinos, from Atlantic City to Vegas, *Rounders* effectively creates an alternative universe in which only the game matters.

Edward Norton, Matt Damon and John Turturro guarding chip stacks in *Rounders*.

♦ ♣ ♥ ♠

Matt Damon is a law student who returns to hustling poker to help a friend, Ed Norton, out of a huge debt. Lots of poker action and *bon mots*, and on the way Damon rediscovers his love of the buzz. Johnny Chan plays himself when Damon recounts to another rounder how he bluffed him out of a pot in Atlantic City. John Turturro is superb as a hardened, cynical grafter at the tables, while John Malkovich oozes cool menace as a Russian heavy-hitter. The film that inspired Chris Moneymaker, and a whole generation, to take up the game.

The Gambler Dick Lowry, 1983

Although one might hesitate to recommend this made-for-TV-movie, and its two spin-offs, it nevertheless briefly held the title of the most-watched TV movie ever, featured charismatic C&W singer Kenny Rogers in a career-making acting role, and was based on his most successful single. Hokum, yes, but look out for suave Bruce Boxleitner (in all three films) and, in *Part II*, tight-jeaned Linda Evans as the fastest female 'slinger in the West.

> *"You got to know when to hold 'em, know*
> *when to fold 'em."*

KENNY ROGERS, THE GAMBLER, 1983

California Split Robert Altman, 1974

Starring Elliott Gould and George Segal as two gambling addicts, this film shows the sometime drudgery of being a professional gambler, moving from cards to horses, sleeping until noon before getting up to find some action, gradually demythologizing the 'glamour' of gambling in the same way as Altman attacked the military (in *M*A*S*H*, 1969), the music industry (in *Nashville*, 1975)

and fashion (in *Prêt à Porter*, 1994). Amarillo Slim has a guest role in the film. Altman shows the attractions of gambling but also the fear, despite the fact that the two men predominantly win. Importantly, Altman does not judge or moralize, but rather lets the games play. Gould's reappearance in Steven Soderberg's *Ocean's 11* and *Ocean's 12* confirmed his status as a celebrity gambler.

Cheyenne Autumn John Ford, 1964
A bit of a cheat to include this, as Ford's elegiac Western, made as an apology for the way he had treated the Indians in previous films, devotes a mere four minutes of its monumental 170-minute running time to poker. But, in an amusing cameo scene, James Stewart plays an aging but elegant Wyatt Earp who, rudely interrupted at his game, shoots his antagonist through the table. Then calmly continues his game. Perfect.

Havana Sydney Pollack, 1990
Robert Redford is a high-stakes gambler who chases the big pots as Batista's Cuba succumbs to the revolutionaries in 1958. Throw in the love interest with a wife of a revolutionary for standard Hollywood

Robert Redford playing it cool in the overheated *Havana*.

fare. One superb line by Redford contrasts politics with poker, explaining how politicians cannot understand how it is sometimes worth losing a pot to set up a much bigger win later.

House of Games David Mamet, 1987

An intricate psychological mystery, playwright Mamet's debut directorial film sees a female psychiatrist confronting a cardsharp for a big-money game in order to clear a suicidal patient's debts. A claustrophobic and haunting film, Mamet explores the similarities between the two individuals – both trade on understanding human nature and trust – despite the somewhat stylized and stilted theatrical presentation.

Things getting wildly out of hand in *House of Games*.

♦ ♣ ♥ ♠

WINNERS
AND LOSERS

THE POKER GREATS

Into the Lion's Den

Any list of the all-time poker greats will inevitably cause controversy. The WSOP Hall of Fame (see page 246) is a case in point, and every enthusiast is capable of building their own pantheon of his or her favourite players. Anyway, here goes, from the great and the good to the new professionals and a celebrity player or two.

The Veterans

These are the guys who built the foundations upon which the modern game is played, the first players to take the step from travelling poker sharps to become professionals at the tables in Las Vegas, stars in their own right, and stalwarts of the WSOP.

Johnny Moss, 'The Grand Old Man of Poker'

Amarillo Slim may be the most celebrated poker player ever, but Johnny Moss, who died in 1997 at the age of 90, is regarded as one of the greatest. He won three of the first five WSOP main event titles while in his 60s, and would probably have won more had old age not got in his way. It didn't stop him playing, though, and between 1970 and 1995, Moss took part in every WSOP, picking up eight titles in all and winning over $680,000 in tournament play.

The most famous story about Moss comes from 1949, when Las Vegas gambling mogul Benny Binion set him up in a marathon five-month long poker game with Nick 'The Greek' Dandolos, another legendary player from this era (see opposite). Nobody seems to know for sure, but it's generally accepted that Moss took somewhere between $2 million and $4 million from Dandolos during this epic, after which Dandolos uttered one of the most famous poker lines ever: 'Mr Moss, I have to let you go.'

♦ ♣ ♥ ♠

Moss was a Texan from the town of Odessa and it was here that he learned to gamble as a young boy. He was taught how to cheat in card games and Moss put this knowledge to good use when, as a teenager, he was hired by a local saloon to watch over games and ensure they were played fairly. It wasn't long before he became a rounder, touring America for the best gambling action, and a strong advocate of Texas Hold'em.

> *'Hold 'em is to stud what chess is to checkers.'*
>
> JOHNNY MOSS

One time Moss was playing in Oklahoma when he spotted a peephole in the ceiling being used to spy on the cards, the information being relayed to another player at the table. Moss, who always packed iron at the time, threatened to shoot the man in the ceiling and, when ignored, ended up wounding him.

One of the first high-profile gamblers, Moss was never very far from danger and made no secret of his Mafia connections. He openly admitted staying at the Las Vegas Flamingo casino and hotel for a number of years at the expense of its owner, famous mobster Benjamin 'Bugsy' Siegal. But it was Benny Binion who became Moss's greatest benefactor over the years, helping to make him the legend he is. In 1979, Moss was a charter inductee to the WSOP Poker Hall of Fame and the starting hand Ace-Ten is sometimes called the 'Johnny Moss' in his honour.

Nick 'The Greek' Dandolos
Dandolos will go down in history as the man who lost up to $4 million dollars to Johnny Moss in 1949 in a single mammoth game of poker lasting five months (see opposite). But it should be

remembered that he didn't always lose – he won some enormous pots too. He had come to Las Vegas in 1949 from the East Coast, having purportedly won tens of millions of dollars from playing craps and poker. He was a 57-year-old gambler in search of the ultimate poker game. Nearly all casinos in those days put limits on the amount players could bet, but Dandolos wanted to play a no-limit game that was the 'biggest this world had to offer'. He approached Benny Binion, who set him up against Johnny Moss – and the rest is history.

> *'The next best thing to gambling and winning is gambling and losing,'*

NICK 'THE GREEK' DANDOLOS

While Dandolos was an inveterate gambler who eventually bankrupted himself, he was also a charming, intelligent and incredibly well-read man. He was renowned for quoting Aristotle and Plato and even claimed to have a philosophy degree from an English university, although nobody has ever discovered which one.

Born in Crete, Dandolos is known to have been educated at a Greek Evangelical College in the Turkish town of Smyrna (now Izmir). The son of a rug merchant and the nephew of a wealthy ship owner, he was sent to America in 1911 at the age of 18. He soon took to gambling, winning and losing huge sums on horse-racing, dice and card games.

He became a student of casino games, however, and in a few years was a huge attraction when at the tables – partly because he would seldom stop gambling even after losing, as he frequently did, as much as $100,000 in a single session. Stories about Dandolos

abound. He claims to have bankrupted East Coast gambling king
Arnold Rothstein – the man who fixed the World Series in 1919
– although this is hard to believe. However, other tales don't seem
quite so tall: he is thought to have once won a city block in Los
Angeles; challenged an arrogant opponent to draw one card for
$550,000 (the other man backed down); and to have once gambled
for 10 days and nights solidly without sleep.

Despite these Herculean feats, at the end of his career Dandolos was
almost penniless, playing low-limit poker in Southern California.
Asked how he could bet millions of dollars once and now play for
$5 chips, Dandolos said: 'Hey, it's action.' He died in 1966, and was
made a charter inductee to the WSOP Poker Hall of Fame in 1979.

Thomas Austin Preston, 'Amarillo Slim'
He is probably the most famous poker player ever, who succeeded
becoming a star in his own right long before the game had captured
the popular imagination. No other person has done as much to
bring poker to the masses, and his influence on the current boom
should not be underestimated.

The exposure started in 1972 when Slim won the main event at
the third WSOP, held at Benny Binion's Horseshoe casino in Las
Vegas. After capturing first prize, Slim embarked on a PR-drive,
appearing on successive television shows, promoting the game,
himself and his new friend Binion's casino. In this media blitz, Slim
managed to have an entire episode *The Tomorrow Show* devoted to
himself and Binion. There followed appearances on Johnny Carson's
Tonight Show, Good Morning America, 60 Minutes and many others.
Such was his fame that he also won a cameo part playing himself
alongside George Segal and Elliott Gould in the Robert Altman
movie *California Split* (1974).

As a result of this publicity, Amarillo Slim became a household name in 1970s America. This was no small achievement for a middle-aged Texan (brought up in Amarillo,) who had started out as a pool hustler and made his living entirely from gambling, touring the country with the likes of Johnny Moss looking for card games. Since those days, Slim has won a total of four WSOP titles, and more than $500,000 in tournament play. He was inducted into the Poker Hall of Fame in 1992.

Everywhere you look in Slim's life you find colour. People working for drugs baron Pablo Escobar once kidnapped him when he was invited to open a casino in Colombia. In his autobiography, *Amarillo Slim in a World Full of Fat People* (2003), he revealed tales of playing poker with *Hustler* publisher Larry Flynt, and presidents Lyndon Johnson and Richard Nixon.

This colour sometimes turns dark, though, and Slim's life has not been short of controversy. He has been labelled a chauvinist – after having been quoted (some say falsely) saying that if a woman ever won the WSOP he'd slit his throat – and anti-Semitic, following remarks on a radio show that scuppered a movie deal tied to his book. Worse than any of this, though, was his 2003 indictment on three charges of indecency with his 12-year-old granddaughter. The charges were reduced to misdemeanour assault in a plea-bargain, and in February 2004 he pleaded guilty to them, receiving a $4000 fine and two years 'deferred adjudication'.

Doyle Brunson

'Texas Dolly', as he is affectionately known, is a colossus of poker, both at the table and in the boardroom. Early in 2005 he launched an audacious $700 million cash bid for the World Poker Tour. His best-selling book, *Super System*, remains one of the finest guides

Ruthless at the felt but generous and charming off it, Brunson is the current Godfather of poker.

to the game; it has since been updated to Super System 2. He has a poker column syndicated throughout the world and his own online poker site – doylesroom.com – is one of the fastest-growing in a highly competitive field.

Yet he still he finds time to play the highest-stakes poker at the Bellagio in Las Vegas and win the 2004 Legends of Poker WPT event. To be a great, though, means winning the big one, the WSOP main event, and Brunson has won it twice, in 1976 and 1977, with the same hand, Ten-Two, which is known today as the 'Doyle Brunson' hand. In total he has ten WSOP bracelets, but he may never have played poker seriously if he had not suffered a terrible knee injury.

Born in 1933, and brought up in Texas, he spent most of his youth playing sports. Such was his prowess that he was an NBA draft for the Minneapolis Lakers until his knee injury curtailed his sports career. Disappointed with the paltry pay cheque from his one and only regular job, Brunson became a rounder, seeking poker games throughout Texas with sidekick Amarillo Slim. Robbed on many occasions, and frustrated with Texas gamblers shutting him out because he won too much, Brunson was drawn to Las Vegas.

♦ ♣ ♥ ♠

A committed Christian, Brunson is one of the most honourable gamblers, and indeed he has frequently stated that gambling should be considered a profession and have a code of ethics where honour and a man's word are his bond. His lack of ego is partly attributed to the death of his daughter, Doyla, when she was aged 18, but a son, Todd, may soon be challenging the 'old man' at the tables.

> *I'm a gambler. I'll always be one. I couldn't be anything else. So, my life will always be full of wins and losses. I wouldn't have it any other way. It's exciting. There's never been a dull moment in my life.*

DOYLE BRUNSON

Walter Clyde 'Puggy' Pearson

'Puggy' or 'Pug' (as he is known due to his stubbed nose) is considered one of poker's finest. His story is of a kid who learned to hustle his way from abject poverty in Tennessee, where he was born during the Depression in 1929, to having a camper van – the 'Rovin Gambler' – in which he toured the States with the motto on the side, 'I'll play any man from any land any game he can name for any amount he can count' – and then in very fine print, 'Provided I like it'.

For over 25 years, Pug played in the highest-stake games he could find, often shouting 'Deal me in!' for the highest game as he entered the room without actually knowing what the game was.

His greatest moment was defeating Johnny Moss, in the 1973 WSOP, when his Ace high with a Flush draw stood up against Moss's

♦ ♣ ♥ ♠

Straight draw. It was a deserved win, as it was he and Benny Binion that had seen the dramatic potential of a freeze-out tournament.

His aptitude for gambling flourished during his first stint in the navy, aged 16, where he made money at cards and pool, but when he learned of the potential for hustling at golf he learned and practised until he became a scratch golfer. On the greens, where sometimes rounds would be worth over $100,000, he was notorious for being a brilliant putter. So much so that one day, when asked which golfer he would choose to make a putt for his life, Johnny Moss ignored the professionals on the PGA Tour and plumped for Pearson instead.

Pearson was only the second living person to be inducted into the WSOP Poker Hall of Fame, in 1987.

Jack 'Treetops' Straus

The 1982 WSOP champion, 'Treetops' – he was over 6 ft 6 ins tall – was inducted into the WSOP Poker Hall of Fame in 1988, having died of a heart attack during a high-stakes poker game at the Bicycle casino in southern California in August that year. He was only 58 years old, and it was ironic that a fearless gambler known for his huge 'heart' at the table was let down by his own blood pump.

> *'I can get all the money I need to gamble on,*
> *but I have hell paying my rent.'*

JACK STRAUS

Even among the poker and gambling fraternity – Straus was a huge punter on sports as well as cards – he was renowned for his desire to gamble. He betted on a wide number of sports, in addition to his career at the poker table, which sometimes left him short of funds, though it was at the poker table that he tended to recoup his losses. In 1982, en route to the WSOP title, Straus thought he was busted out when he had one single chip worth $500 left. He played it, went on a roll and won the entire event. In truth, Straus was a better cash player than tournament player, although Straus still won two WSOP bracelets.

He was also a keen traveller and hunter. On a safari to Mozambique he shot a lion and put its paw on a keychain, his motto from then on being 'Better a day as a lion than a lamb for a hundred years.'

The Young Guns
The 1980s and 1990s saw the emergence of a new generation of poker superstars, young, talented, determined and unafraid to take on their seniors – and win.

Johnny Chan
Johnny Chan, or the 'Orient Express' as he is affectionately known, is one of the modern legends of poker, and was the first of the new wave of younger stars. He held a record ten WSOP winners' bracelets – until Doyle Brunson matched his total in 2005– has won two consecutive WSOP $10,000 No-Limit Hold'em events in 1987 and 1988 – this time mimicking Brunson – and nearly won it a third time when he came second to Phil Hellmuth Jnr. in 1989.

When the film *Rounders* was being shot in 1998 and they wanted some footage and scenes with a real-life professional, it was Chan they featured, playing himself. But, in a world where names are made by money and tournaments won, Chan deserves his title as one of the best ever poker players by achievement on the felt.

♦ ♣ ♥ ♠

Born in Hong Kong, Chan moved to Phoenix, Arizona in 1968 and from there to Houston, Texas where his family owned restaurants. Ironic really that if he had pursued his family business he could have been filling tables rather than emptying them.

In the early 1980s he started playing poker, mastered every type of major game and it is testament to his all-round ability that his WSOP bracelets cover six different events: No-Limit Hold'em, Texas Hold'em, Pot-Limit Hold'em, Seven-Card Stud, Pot-Limit Omaha and Deuce-to-Seven Draw.

A player of great consistency, another constant feature is the orange he places on the table by his chips. Considered by many to be a lucky charm, Chan has said that he likes the smell and it helps dispel the aroma of cigarette smoke.

Like many players he has parlayed his poker prowess and winnings into solid investments, notably restaurants. It seems that Chan's life is destined to revolve around tables of whatever kind. The respect that he has in the poker world was demonstrated in 2002, when he was the first Asian American to gain a place in the WSOP Poker Hall of Fame in 2002.

Phil Ivey

One of the modern poker superstars, Ivey is as famous for his nickname – the 'Tiger Woods' of poker – as for his dignity when suffering a bad beat. Ivey grew up in New Jersey and started playing casino games aged 17. Atlantic City was his first poker battleground, but with the age limit for casinos being 21, Ivey spent his first four years playing in Atlantic City with a fake ID and name, Jerome Graham. Like so many of his generation brought up on computer games, he was an exceptional gamer before finding poker.

Jerome Graham? Tiger Woods? Can Phil Ivey figure out whose chips these are?

Ivey initially came to a wider public prominence with his first WSOP bracelet wins in 2000, when he defeated Phil Hellmuth Jnr. and Amarillo Slim in the Pot-Limit Omaha tournament. Seen as a new kid on the block at the time (Ivey was in fact only 20 years old at the time) two years later he confirmed his all-round poker ability by winning three more bracelets, then equalling the record of wins at the WSOP in a single year.

He looked likely to go one better and win the big one the following year, 2003 – the $10,000 No -Limit Hold'em event but Chris Moneymaker, the eventual winner, outdrew him with a stronger Full House knocking him out in 10th position.

In 2005, Ivey reached two World Poker Tour final tables and secured his fifth WSOP bracelet by winning the $5000 Pot- Limit Omaha tournament.

Like many professionals enjoying the current boom in poker, Ivey has translated his table success into business enterprises and is one of the major professionals behind the online poker site – www.fulltiltpoker.com.

With so many players today wearing sunglasses to mask any tells their eyes may give away to opponents, it is interesting that on the only occasion Ivey tried them he misread his hand. In anger he threw the $1100 glasses in the bin - their true cost the $100,000 pot that he lost.

♦ ♣ ♥ ♠

Gus Hansen

Gus Hansen, aka the 'Great Dane', is one of the most aggressive No-Limit Hold'em poker players around today, a point shown on numerous occasions on TV when such famous players like Doyle Brunson have shaken their heads and wondered aloud exactly what hand Hansen is playing. This is because Hansen is an all-action player, keener on putting pressure on his opponents and forcing them call a substantial bet than folding tamely while waiting for a monster hand.

It is a style that has worked for the Dane, but despite such a loose reputation at the felt, he is an analytical player. A background as a ranked backgammon player in Denmark player informs his approach to poker. His opponents have observed that he plays a lot of rag hands, but plays them perfectly. Hansen instead refers to the established backgammon philosophy of 'equity', the expectation of profit off a hand if it is played an infinite number of times. This may account for his aggressive and successful poker style.

In 2004, Gus Hansen was voted one of the '50 Sexiest Men' by *People Magazine*, alongside the usual hunk suspects like Jude Law, Johnny Depp and Brad Pitt. Not surprisingly, he is the poker babes' favourite player.

In the first two seasons of the World Poker Tour Hansen won three titles, and was the leading money-winner, earning nearly $2 million. These results brought him the accolade of being one of the first three inductees into the WPT Hall of Fame, alongside Doyle Brunson and maverick actor James Garner, in 2005.

What is more, despite his aggressive poker style, he is considered by most other players as a genuinely friendly man. Like many other top-line players, Hansen is also involved in a poker online site, www.pokerchamps.com.

Phil Hellmuth Jr.

When 24-year-old university dropout Phil Hellmuth Jr. pitched up at the WSOP in 1989, he was unheard of. By the end of the tournament he had become the youngest person ever to win the title, kick-starting a career that would see him reach the top of the game. He has since won nine WSOP titles, has the most WSOP Poker Hall of Fame tournament wins and was voted the 'Greatest Living Poker Player' by his peers in 1996.

But his success has not come without controversy, and Hellmuth's antics over the years have led to him being dubbed the 'Poker Brat'. He has great difficulty accepting bad luck when it comes his way, and his child-like temper tantrums at the table are infamous. Hellmuth can't seem to resist throwing his huge 6ft 5ins frame to the floor, flailing his arms about and whining like a spoiled kid when he's beaten by a hand he deems unworthy. Even appearing on television isn't enough to calm his behaviour, and Hellmuth's histrionics have been caught on camera on numerous occasions; it can make for compelling viewing, particularly when opponents try to wind him up.

As well as being moody, Hellmuth is also perceived by others as having a massive ego. While his stated life's ambition is to become the 'greatest poker player who ever lived', many believe he already thinks he is – although, to be fair, his record does justify his arrogance.

Despite his massive success Hellmuth is playing less and less poker these days. Now married with two children, and living in suburban California, he has become a franchise having written two books, starred in a series of DVDs and started a clothing line. He has also launched a mobile phone game, is in negotiations over a reality-TV series based around himself, writes a variety of newspaper and magazine columns and has had a doll modelled on him. His poker-related business activities are, in Hellmuth's own words, just too lucrative to ignore.

> *'If there weren't luck involved,*
> *I guess I'd win every one.'*

PHIL HELLMUTH JR.

To cap it all, for a cool $25,000 he can be lured away from his busy schedule. For this fee Hellmuth can be hired to come to your house to give you head-to-head lessons, after which he will run a tournament for you and 200 of your closest pals.

Joseph Hachem

When 39-year-old Joseph Hachem hit his straight in the final hand of the 2005 WSOP main event, he became the first Australian poker champion of the world (see pages 184-185). He also became the first winner for three years to have paid up the $10,000 buy-in fee, the previous two years' final tables being won by Online qualifiers. But Hachem was as much an unknown quantity as any other recent winner – the 2005 WSOP being the first he had ever entered.

He is no poker professional. While he says he plays as regularly as possible at a professional level, he has a day job as a mortgage broker, a line of work he has followed since a condition he developed

THE STUEY UNGAR STORY

When Stuey Ungar's cold, lifeless body was discovered sprawled on the bed in Room 16 at the Oasis Motel in Las Vegas on Sunday November 22, 1998 the erratic, frequently turbulent life of the man who many regarded as the greatest poker player to have ever lived had come to a sadly predictable and tragic end.

Struggling with a drug addiction for many years, his unconventional lifestyle and dependence on substances like crack had finally proved too much for his frail body. The coroner stated after the autopsy that 'the cause is accidental death by coronary atherosclerosis. The heart condition developed over a period of time. The death was brought on by his lifestyle.'

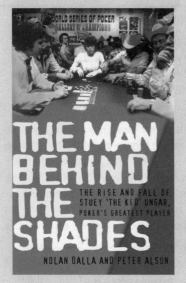

The tragic high-rolling life of Stuey Ungar reads like the text of a novel. The bestselling *The Man Behind the Shades* (2005) is a factual account of his extraordinary life.

♦ ♣ ♥ ♠

In truth, the seeds of his demise had been sown many years before; as a child when he would skip school and help his father, Ido, run a betting shop from his bar. It became a favoured haunt in the 1950s of wiseguys and gamblers, exposing the young Ungar to a seedy underworld of crime and limited responsibility.

It was one of the mobsters, Victor Romano, who tried to nurture Ungar after his father had died. Ungar had already caused a stir in the card rooms of New York by defeating some well-known gin rummy players and, with Romano's backing and support, other matches were set up along the East Coast. Ungar was staked by Romano, thereby effectively becoming a Mob employee – which also gave him protection.

He played in Miami and won. In fact everywhere Ungar played he won, due to an extraordinary photographic memory for cards and his clinical scrutiny of his opponents. One notable bet he won was with his friends, who dealt out four packs of cards leaving the last card unturned. Ungar correctl;y identified it as the Ten of Diamonds.

Ungar's extraordinary skills were blended with ungracious manners; he would rather humiliate an opponent than let them think they had a chance, which meant he would keep playing, losing more. This irritated his paymasters which, combined with his inability to control his winnings, forced him to flee temporarily to California in 1978.

His problem was not earning money – his skill at gin rummy and knack of learning a new game in an evening and then winning at it from then on, proved that. However, what he could not do was stop gambling it all at the racetrack. Ungar was not just a magnificent talent at cards, a fearless opponent with apparently no regard for money, but a degenerate gambler who craved action at all times.

STU UNGAR continued

Later in 1978 he arrived in Las Vegas, won as usual at gin rummy and then discovered poker. For a man obsessed with high-stakes gambling he was drawn to no limit Hold'em. His first entry into the WSOP was 1980, and it was then that the poker legend of Stu Ungar was born.

The foundation of the legend was his win-ratio in big tournaments with a buy-in of $5000 or more. In total he won ten no limit Hold'em titles, including both the WSOP and the other huge tournament of the time, Amarillo Slim's Super Bowl of Poker. In fact, he won both the WSOP and the Super Bowl three times, a record which has never been beaten.

But the first was that WSOP in 1980. With his mentor, Romano, in the crowd watching, Ungar won through to the final heads-up confrontation with Doyle Brunson. It was Ungar, the 'Kid', against the twice-world champion. Most observers gave Ungar no chance, including a bookmaker at the event. When the bookie shouted Ungar's odds at 6:5, the 'Kid' put $45,000 on himself. Hearing this, Brunson immediately declared that he would lay the bet himself. Not only were they playing for the championship, but there was a substantial side wager and pride at stake.

In the end it was the unrated Ungar who won when he flopped the 'nuts'. In the ensuing mayhem he was asked by a reporter what he would do with the $365,000 prize. Ungar, bemused by such a question, answered simply (and honestly): 'Gamble it.'

And he did, but not until he had first registered a Social Security number. The 'Kid' from New York was now the world champion with light bulbs flashing in his face and a fistful of money but he was not recognized by the government. Neither did he have a bank account. The money that survived the celebratory party went into safe deposit boxes around Las Vegas. Ominously, Ungar's father figure

♦ ♣ ♥ ♠

and mentor failed to survive the celebratory party. After the party, Romano complained of indigestion, and the next day he was dead.

In 1981, Ungar was preparing to defend his WSOP title in the main event, the $10,000 No Limit Hold'em, but an altercation with a dealer just days before the event started put his entry in jeopardy. During an argument some saliva from Ungar's mouth hit the dealer. Whether it was deliberate or not is debatable but Benny Binion banned him from the Horseshoe and it was only the intervention of Jack Binion, Benny's son, that saw Ungar's entry reinstated. What he did then was simple – he won. By the age of 27 he was a double world champion and fêted as an all-time great.

The rest of the 1980s however proved challenging for Ungar. He developed dangerous drug habits, gambled huge sums, winning and losing equally. He was living in the fast lane. On one magnificent day he went to a race meeting and won $1.6 million. The 1980s also saw the birth of a daughter, Stephanie, and the adoption of a son, Richie. But later, he was divorced from his wife, Madeleine and Richie, while living with Ungar in Las Vegas, became depressed and, in 1989, committed suicide.

By 1997 Ungar was barely considered a serious contender any longer, but an old friend, Billy Baxter, staked him at the last minute for the WSOP and Ungar, in probably his finest moment, won the tournament once again.

A chance for redemption had presented itself but was spurned as 12 months later he failed to defend his title, retreated further into the drugs that had overtaken his life and then died, aged 45, alone and penniless in November of that year.

For a man who is reputed to have won over $30 million, it was an ignoble end; the collection at the service was needed to pay for the funeral.

in his hands forced him to retire from being a chiropractor. Also, he is every bit the committed family man, having stated that his responsibilities to his wife and four children (three boys and one girl) were what had previously stopped him from entering the poker world's biggest event.

But in the months leading up to the 2005 event, he got the green light to head to Nevada. 'It had been a dream of mine to enrol in the WSOP for a long time,' said Hachem in the days after winning. 'This year my wonderful wife suggested I go to Vegas with my friends and try my luck. And here I am!'

So how did he achieve the dream of winning $7.5million first prize? 'During the preliminaries, I played each day as a separate tournament, and set my goals each session and each day,' he said. 'There was a period when I was short-stacked for 11 hours, which meant I was at risk of elimination on every hand. Keeping my concentration for so long was the hardest task of my life, but I managed it!'

Hachem didn't just use concentration though – he admits he had some luck on his side. One of the photographers at the event gave him a lucky penny early on during the final table. 'I kept it in my back pocket the whole time. At each break the guy who gave it to me would check up on me...which was really cool.'

Ladies at the Table

When WSOP launched over thirty years ago the notion of women playing, let alone contending seriously, would have been treated with derision and even scorn. Aside from the machismo associated with cool cardplay, somehow the heart, aggression and ruthlessness necessary to compete at the highest level were assumed to be attributes which women were unlikely to possess. Today, however, the poker room is no longer the preserve of men, and a generation of highly-skilled female players has arrived.

Annie Duke

Considered as the finest female poker player in the world, Annie Duke has proved herself one of the all-time greats with her victory in the WSOP Champions event in 2004. The only female in the invitation-only tournament, she knocked out Phil Hellmuth Jnr., Phil Ivey, Daniel Negreanu, T.J. Cloutier, Johnny Chan and the man who introduced her to poker back in the early 1990s, her brother Howard Lederer. Her prize? A cool $2 million and further bragging rights over Lederer.

Growing up Duke was a student more than a card player. She majored in English and Psychology at Columbia University and continued studying Cognitive Psychology at the University of Pennsylvania but, encouraged by her brother and her results in poker games back in her home state of Montana, she entered the World Series in 1994.

When Phil Hellmuth Jnr talks it is frequently about himself, but he described Annie Duke as: 'The best all round woman poker player in the world today!'

♦ ♣ ♥ ♠

Her results as a debutante were astonishing: 13th in her first
tournament and third in her second, but it was only in 2004 that
she earned the most coveted trophy, a WSOP winner's bracelet for
the $2000 buy-in Omaha High-Low event. Clearly her skills cover
most poker games: twice she has placed second in the Limit Hold'em
events at the WSOP, and she won the $2500 Limit Hold'em at the
Bellagio, making her the first woman to win two major events in the
same year.

> *'Poker is one of the only games where a*
> *woman can compete on a totally equal footing*
> *with a man – so I don't understand why there*
> *are Ladies-only tournaments.'*

ANNIE DUKE

Interestingly, for a lady determined to mix it with the men, she has
raised a family of four children, admitted that if the choice were one
of the kid's plays or a poker game, the play would win. Any who see
Duke at the table though, one leg tucked up on the seat, and think
she is weak are badly mistaken. On numerous occasions she has
knocked Lederer out of tournaments, and those that have witnessed
these on television will remember her wry smile, slight inclination of
the head towards him as he stands up to leave, and then her busy
gathering of his chips.

Jennifer Tilly
Actors and actresses are supposed to covet Golden Globes and
Oscars. They are the measure of their achievement -but no longer
for Jennifer Tilly. She has been nominated for the best supporting
actress Academy Award for her performance in Woody Allen's

♦ ♣ ♥ ♠

Bullets Over Broadway (1994), but her trophy of choice now is a bracelet, diamond and gold preferably, inscribed with WSOP champion.

And, since June 2005, when she shut out 600 other hopefuls in the Ladies Only $1000 No-Limit Hold'em event she can claim both to being a world champion and the first movie star to make the transition to fully-fledged poker winner.

Her game was helped by being taught by her partner Phil Laak, the exceptional player known as the 'Unabomber', which in turn helped Tilly graduate from the celebrity poker circuit (where she met Laak) to the highest echelons of poker. The $158,000 that she won should keep her a fixture in other tournaments for some time, and her sentiment that winning the WSOP bracelet was 'better than winning an Oscar' endeared her to the poker fraternity.

Stars in Their Own Right: Celebrity Players
There is no reason of course why anybody from any walk of life cannot play, and become expert at poker, and indeed many do. But there has always been an interesting area of overlap between showbiz and the poker table – both worlds share the glitz and glamour, and the luxury trappings that success can bring.

Telly Savalas
Veteran movie star and of course television's most popular cop, Kojak himself, it would be wrong to think of Savalas as an actor in this book, but rather as a bona fide poker player.

'Who loves ya, baby?' and as slick at the table as on screen.

A regular at the WSOP during the 1980s and an almost constant figure at tables in both Los Angeles and Las Vegas throughout the rest of the year, Savalas, according to many who played against, him had great presence at the table, with an impressively impassive game face. Maybe not surprising for a man who studied Psychology at Columbia University and won a Purple Heart during World War II. And, as noted early, an ability to act is also a great asset at the poker table. It certainly worked as his best place finish in the WSOP was in

OCEAN'S 11

When Lewis Milestone's film *Ocean's 11* was released in 1960, with Sinatra and his Clan capering around the Sands casino, planning to heist three casinos simultaneously seemed like the epitome of cool. Gambling had come out of the shadows, and in the ensuing years of the Kennedys, *Playboy* magazine, and annual James Bond movies, ability at the gaming tables became an important attribute of the suave, cool man-about-town. But in the Rat Pack film, precious little gambling took place.

Steven Soderbergh's remake 41 years later, starring George Clooney, Brad Pitt, Andy Garcia, Elliott Gould and Julia Roberts, repeated the formula, with less spoofing around, a more credible plot and the most glamorous stars of the day. The same team went on to make *Ocean's 12*, set in Europe. However, the real action took place off set. Most nights Soderbergh, Elliott Gould, Pitt, Don Cheadle, Casey Affleck, Michael Douglas and Matt Damon would get together for Texas Hold'em. Clooney declined, believing luck was against him at the table, and settled for the role of drinks waiter, but Pitt (who has made no secret of his passion for the game) and Gould (who had also featured in Robert Altman's *California Split* in 1974) emerged as the most serious players, constantly going head

♦ ♣ ♥ ♠

1992 when he came in 21st in the $10,000 No-Limit Hold'em event. Many online reports and blogs have stories of playing against him at Hold'em and Seven-Card Stud, and all mention his impenetrable aura at the table. And as the cop with the cute catchphrase, he almost had to have some one-liners at the felt. 'Pussycats', he growled at his starting table at the WSOP main event one year - a table that included Stu Ungar.

to head. With the buy-in a reputed 50 euros neither was likely to be busted whichever way it went.

in 2005 George Clooney teamed up with Brad Pitt to open their own casino.

Mimi Rogers
A Hollywood home-game specialist and board member of the WPT since 2004, Rogers is known as an astute player but the veteran actress, constantly in demand on screen since her 1981 debut in *Hill Street Blues*, has failed so far to translate that success on to the baize.

She is a regular on the celebrity poker circuit and in February 2005 came closest to a major final when she survived down to the final three of the celebrity tournament at the WPT Invitational at the Commerce Casino in Los Angeles.

Actress Mimi Rogers at the pro-celeb London Open in 2005

From a starting field of 40 celebrity contestants, Rogers ended up battling it out with Hill Harper of CSI/NY fame and the eventual winner, Tom Everett Scott, star of *That Thing You Do*. Scott's prize was a seat the final table of the main event, in which nearly 200 professionals were competing.

For Rogers it may have been a case of 'so near and yet so far', but being a player and executive in poker is really a natural extension from her teenage years. She worked as a volunteer in charity groups

♦ ♣ ♥ ♠

and, when the opportunity arose, travelled with her card-playing father to Lake Tahoe to join in at the poker and blackjack tables. A schooling that has benefited her later life. Who needs a college education when you can play cards?

Ben Affleck

Ben Affleck made history in 2004 when he became the first film celebrity to win a major poker championship. The Hollywood heartthrob and star of films such as *Good Will Hunting* and *Armageddon* finished first in the $10,000 buy-in California State Poker Championship, scooping more than $350,000. This makes him the only person in the world to have both an Academy Award and a major poker championship to his name.

So all the money he spent on coaching paid off. Whereas most of us had to learn to play the game from books and bitter experience, Affleck paid top players to teach him their tricks and even regularly flew his first coach, Amir Vahedi, to lessons on his private jet. To finish the job of turning him into a top poker player, Affleck approached one of the best female professionals on the circuit, Annie Duke, who subsequently honed his skills, transforming him into the championship-winner he is.

Affleck is by all accounts an avid student of the game and has won respect from poker professionals who now recognize him as a worthy adversary. Apparently he has great poker instincts and doesn't just play for the money. With his bankroll, though, you wouldn't have to.

ANATOMY OF
A POKER PRO

Going Pro?

If you are thinking that poker offers the chance of a get-rich-quick future of untold riches, think again. All of the great professional players have served their time at the tables; in the past, rounders like Johnny Moss, Amarillo Slim and 'Puggy' Pearson spent many years travelling from one town to another, sniffing out the good games, chancing their arm, and learning by their mistakes. It was a Colt 45 in the waistband, sawed-off scattergun in the trunk, and an Ace-up-the-sleeve kind of existence. Today things have changed: now almost anyone can enter a big tournament through Internet qualifying rounds, and if they hit the money spots they automatically become celebrities, feted like Hollywood stars; but even these guys and girls have had to earn their chops through dedicating thousands of hours at the table or in front of a screen.

What are the attributes needed to make a good poker player, even a professional? Weight, height, athleticism – in poker none of these qualities would seem to matter. The important attributes which do seem common to most successful players have more to do with character and temperament, plus a head for figures.

It has been said that great gamblers are born, not made - but much the same could be said for outstanding sportsmen in other fields. While it is true that you can't change your character, it is possible to modify your behaviour, and it is also possible to develop various skills which will certainly improve your game. We have already identified certain useful aspects of playing - self-knowledge, observation and concentration - in the chapter on the Psychology of Poker (pages 116-118). Here we look at the skills you can concentrate on, hone and develop to increase the chances of making a profit – indeed possibly a living – from playing poker.

Patience

For most of us poker is a game played at night. The bigger poker tournaments span several days, and games can extend into the small hours. Without a doubt the single most important ability is to be able to sit through hours of gaming without losing concentration or giving in to the inevitable urge to do something rash or impetuous. This requires stamina (albeit of a different order to that required by a long-distance runner) and the ability to stay focussed on what's going on around you. Impatience, irritation, tiredness and simple boredom have lost more hands and more money than any other failings. Patience will develop the more immersed you become in the game, and with it the ability to concentrate on the best way to play.

> *'Poker is a game of many skills: you need card sense, psychological insight, a good memory, controlled aggression, enough mathematical know-how to work out the odds as each hand develops and what poker players call a leather ass – i.e. patience.'*

AL ALVAREZ, *NO LIMITS* (1994)

Know your numbers

A cursory glance through biographies and diaries of star players shows that they would rather base their decisions and hard-earned money on sound principles like mathematics than on the mere luck of the draw. A certain facility with numbers seems to be the first skill that an aspiring pro must master. You might not be the world's best at mental arithmetic, but this is certainly a skill which can be improved.

Of course numbers are not everything, but they are a good foundation. With only 52 cards in a deck, the odds and chances of winning a hand can be calculated pretty well, if not exactly because a few cards remain unseen. It is a point acknowledged by all the good players. Nick 'the Greek' Dandolos adapted a famous slogan by saying 'You can't beat death, taxes and percentages.'

> *'Knowing how to figure the odds will not make a winning player. But a total disregard of the odds for a long period will surely make a loser. Lucky players don't last.'*

A.D. LIVINGSTON

Using mental arithmetic is what the best players do to minimize or manage the effect of luck. They all know luck has a role to play in every hand, but controlling its influence decides how successful they are, and one way of exercising some measure of control is knowing the chances of an event happening - specifically the odds of a card being turned in their favour or, indeed, someone else's.

Self Control and Discipline
Control for a poker player is not only about controlling or minimizing chance. It is also imperative that a player has self control. A bad player will become bored, risk money on poor hands, and wind up a loser. A successful player will wait... and wait...and wait, occasionally playing weak hands so no other player develops a pattern of his play, but still waiting for a strong starting hand to put their chips to work. To achieve this takes discipline and immense resources of self-control, both recurring topics of discussion between good players; with an average of 80% of professional

♦ ♣ ♥ ♠

hands being folded immediately, they certainly have the time to chew over the subject.

> *"It's as important to make good folds in poker as it is to make good bets... The biggest mistake weak players make is playing too many hands."*

AVERY CARDOZA

Controlling the Ego

When a game is being played, many personality habits and traits are accentuated once the cards have been dealt. This means any psychological issues that a player may have will be magnified when playing, and may possibly prove very costly. It is a particular facet of poker that fascinated Al Alvarez: 'I think one of the interesting things about poker is that once you let your ego in, you're done for.'

> *"Big egos and big losses go hand in hand.'*

JOHN GOLLEHON

But this is not to say ego does not play a positive part in poker. Any sport where one competitor wants to destroy another must be based on supremacy and dominance. Either you get your opponent's chips or they get yours, and the best players use their egos wisely, knowing exactly why they are playing as they do, and searching out clues to understanding their opponent's motivations. The key is to spot a player with no understanding or control over theirs, and then to target them. Like everything else in poker, it's a two-way traffic: someone will be watching you as well.

The business of ego is a complex one. Giving too much of yourself away before a game, at the table, or after a game can be critical. In fact, this knowledge is so important to the game that Amarillo Slim went so far as to say that, ultimately, the actual cards dealt didn't really matter. To him it was his opponent that decided who won: 'Poker is a game of people....It's not the hand I hold, it's the people that I play with.'

Aggression

The adversarial aspect of poker attracts many, especially those who go for the jugular in other aspects of their lives. Within most people there is a lust for victory and a warrior spirit, and sport for many provides an outlet for such impulses. But at the poker table, aggression should be regarded as merely a technique, a means of intimidating the opposition, not by snarling at them, but by developing a style of playing which is disconcertingly strong or unpredictable. So don't waste your time practising confrontational role-playing in front of a mirror, like de Niro in *Taxi Driver*. Rather, focus on pursuing a line of play at the table which will unsettle your fellow players.

'Cards are war, in disguise of a sport.'

CHARLES LAMB

Uncontrolled aggression can often scupper many players' hopes of fame and fortune. Knowing when to be aggressive, and being fully committed to it, is very difficult. Stu Ungar could barely control his killer instincts, rashly often reducing his opposition to jelly long before he had milked them of their reserve funds. The other side of

Rhett Butler (Clark Gable) sizes up an opponent in *Gone with the Wind*.

aggression is to play for play's sake, in pursuit of the kill, regardless of the cost. Money? Merely a tool to be used to achieve an end. Great aggressive players, like Phil Hellmuth Jr. and Gus Hanssen, are strong personalities, prepared to challenge opponents rather than fade, but only, shrewdly, when they consider the odds in their favour. Avery Cardoza summed it all up when he said, 'Strong players will sooner raise than call'.

Ruthlessness

And all these ingredients serve one purpose: the urge to win. Every great poker player has never been content when beaten. Winning is an obsession for them, and that demands a ruthless attitude. Whether born with one or having cultivated one, a merciless attitude is ubiquitous among the truly successful. Jack 'Treetops' Straus happily admitted that if he played his grandmother, he'd beat her for every cent. Again, this quality is something that can be nurtured and developed, and it doesn't have to mean that you have to take it away from the table into the rest of your life.

An inability to follow through and destroy your opponent's confidence as you dismantle their chipstacks could prove a fatal weakness. Don't assume they would, under similar circumstances, show you mercy. Don't think of them in a personal manner, but develop the ability to view what you are doing for what it is – playing a game, a game you must win.

Humility: Using Your Down-Time

When great players are all-in, they are decisive and aggressive. When things turn against them, they should be humble enough to turn it to their advantage. While Phil Hellmuth Jr. might make a scene after an ill-judged play or piece of bad luck, this is not for most a role model to be recommended. Having mucked their cards

♦ ♣ ♥ ♠

good players will concentrate on the others, seeking an advantage or tell to utilise later. Learn to lose gracefully, and if you've mucked your hand, use your time profitably by studying your fellow players.

All in all, if you can focus on even some of the features discussed above, especially if you feel that, in your case, they could be improved, you will find the quality your game in turn improves. Whether or not you can turn in the day job is a different matter. But practice is the key to it all: the more you play, the more you will build up a bank of useful experience. And today practice is easy, with so many of the online sites offering schools and tutorials, and providing enough play money games for you to forget about the bankroll. Until you are ready – then go for it.

An old poker saying still rings as it did a century ago 'If you're playing a poker game and you look around the table and can't tell who the sucker is, it's you.'

THE 5 BEST POKER INSTRUCTION BOOKS

Super System *Doyle Brunson* Probably the first and the best course in book form, from the senior statesman of the felt.

Super System 2 *Doyle Brunson* Subtitled 'A Course in Poker Power', it's designed to help you move your game up the ladder.

The Poker Player's Bible *Lou Krieger* A comprehensive treatment from one of the world's foremost player/writers, the book functions both as an exhaustive ready reference and a course.

Deal Me In! *Glenn McDonald* A useful book for online beginners.

Winning Secrets of Online Poker *Douglas W Frye & Curtis D Frye* A book that arrived at just the right time, and brilliantly addresses the specific issues unique to playing the game in cyberspace. Full of useful tips and analysis.

OFF THE RAILS

Courting Lady Luck

Poker may largely be a game of skill requiring a knowledge of human psychology and mathematics to help calculate odds, but still there is an ever-present element of luck or chance.

Sometimes even the best players in the world will get outdrawn, and stories of even the top (let alone over-the-top) players going broke are legion. Legends like Stu Ungar and Puggy Pearson went bust on numerous occasions; they used their reputations to scavenge, beg and borrow a bankroll from somewhere – other poker playing friends usually – to get them playing again, but for most going bust is life changing. It can signal a new, positive direction, or sometimes be life-destroying.

In this modern world where someone, somewhere, is always to blame and morality is enforced, organizations exist to help everybody in everything. Gambling has plenty of support networks and groups and they do very good work for those with a problem. These range from from the world-famous Gambler's Anonymous (GA) to more local networks and Gamcare.

Remember though, no one in poker likes bad beat stories. If you lost a bundle on a bad play, it may not be a gambling problem that requires external help and sympathy. It may just demand a closer study of the game and of the odds. You may simply need to improve your game.

This is not to say that gambling is not addictive. For some it is just like chocolate, alcohol, sex and shopping. The attraction of one last bet, that fulcrum upon which one's entire fortune balances, can for many be irresistible. The idea that ones luck will 'turn' can be just as alluring as that one extra drink or cigarette.

♦ ♣ ♥ ♠

It is easy to say that one plays within one's means, that you know when to back out, but another thing to do it. For many, it is this vital element, tempting fate on a high roll, which proves addictive.

The rapid development of poker online has undoubtedly given cause to widespread reservations about the suitability, and danger, of ready access to a potentially ruinous activity. This, combined with other matrices of the modern global infrastructure (credit lines and credit cards, globalized networks, and exploitation of unregulated systems by organized crime) are entirely legitimate causes for concern. These have been reflected by public debates, notably in the US and UK over regularization, licensing of gaming establishments, and vain attempts to harness the power and access of the Internet. But ultimately, in the developed West at least, we worship at the shrine of competition and individual choice. Self-regulation is the supplication if not the prayer.

One simple self-administered test is to turn the computer off for a couple of days or more and not play any poker at all. If you cannot do that, then you may have a problem and should probably contemplate outside help. If you can manage it, but still lose money when you play, then the problem is your skill level, or your bankroll management. Or maybe you are simply playing in too expensive a game.

Gamblers Anonymous
www.gamblersanonymous.org

Probably the most famous of all self-help groups are those titled 'anonymous'. Gamblers Anonymous (GA) is a global self-help group that started in 1957 when two men met, both of whom were experiencing problems with gambling. The first official GA meeting was on September 13, 1957 in California, and since then the fellowship, as they title it, has grown around the world. There are no charges or fees or subscriptions; funding is derived from voluntary contributions, and GA remains self-sufficient.

On their website, Gamblers Anonymous state that the only requirement for membership is 'a desire to stop gambling'.

There are no political affiliations with GA, and their mission is to help 'compulsive gamblers' who must first acknowledge the existence of a problem and accept that they will never, ever fully control it. That is why GA have regular meetings and a constant support network of 'friends' – all ex-gamblers – on hand to help, to provide counseling and support. Because Gamblers Anonymous believe that those who suffer have a progressive illness, caution every day is their sentiment.

GA have a set of questions that people can access in hard copy or Online. You need to answer these honestly, to gauge whether you do indeed have a problem or a potential problem. GA's line in the sand is about seven positive answers: fewer than this suggests you are a sensible gambler with no need for help or therapy, but much more than seven indicates that gambling is very, possibly unhealthily important to you, and probably dominant in your life.

Honesty in answering these questions is essential, but, like self-knowledge, difficult to achieve. Most obsessive types will instinctively play down their answers while, of course, many successful gamblers will be able to answer yes to many if not most, of the questions. But this is where the buck stops with self-regulation. Best not to judge yourself against others and be absolutely honest.

♦ ♣ ♥ ♠

THE GAMBLERS ANONYMOUS 20 QUESTIONS

- Did you ever lose time from work or school due to gambling?
- Has gambling ever made your home life unhappy?
- Did gambling affect your reputation?
- Have you ever felt remorse after gambling?
- Did you ever gamble to get money with which to pay debts or otherwise solve financial difficulties?
- Did gambling cause a decrease in your ambition or efficiency?
- After losing did you feel you must return as soon as possible and win back your losses?
- After a win did you have a strong urge to return and win more?
- Did you often gamble until your last dollar was gone?
- Did you ever borrow to finance your gambling?
- Have you ever sold anything to finance gambling?
- Were you reluctant to use 'gambling money' for normal expenditures?
- Did gambling make you careless of the welfare of yourself or your family?
- Did you ever gamble longer than you had planned?
- Have you ever gambled to escape worry or trouble?
- Have you ever committed, or considered committing, an illegal act to finance gambling?
- Did gambling cause you to have difficulty in sleeping?
- Do arguments, disappointments or frustrations create within you an urge to gamble?
- Did you ever have an urge to celebrate any good fortune by a few hours of gambling?
- Have you ever considered self destruction or suicide as a result of your gambling?

Most compulsive gamblers will answer yes to seven or more!

♦ ♣ ♥ ♠

Gamcare
www.gamcare.org.uk
helpline: 0845 6000 133

Registered as a charity in the United Kingdom, GAMCARE accepts legal gambling and the freedom of choice of people to pursue such activities, but is concerned with the damage gambling may do to some. Rather than preach, it hopes to help promote responsible attitudes to gambling and to work for the proper care for those affected by gambling.

The Gamcare website and helpline number and offer counselling, advice and fact sheets, and also try to work across many social areas like schools and colleges to educate young people As with Gamblers Anonymous, there is a facility for self-help and self-assessment on their website.

Around the world most countries have counselling services for problem gamblers and indeed many individual US states and the bigger cities do as well.

The National Council on Problem Gambling
www.ncpgambling.org; ncpg@ncpgambling.org
24-hour national helpline: 1 800 522 4700

This is a national service in America to help those afflicted with pathological gambling or problems arising from gambling and all their families. The head office is in Washington but there are state affiliates and a 24-hour confidential national helpline.

♦ ♣ ♥ ♠

THE LISTS

A poker player's address book

It comes as no surprise that the online poker boom has led to a massive increase in the number of people who want to play poker live. It's only natural that those who have played games from the privacy of their homes and then seen the excitement of the televised tournaments should want to experience the buzz of face-to-face encounters over the green baize of a real poker table. And to accommodate this demand, brick and mortar poker rooms in serious decline throughout the 1990s and at risk of disappearing completely, have been opening and reopening everywhere. The world is now awash with places to play so if you fancy it, take your pick from the plethora of global venues listed below.

NORTH AMERICA

USA

ATLANTIC CITY

Borgata
1 Borgata Way, Atlantic City, NJ, 08401
www.theborgata.com

Harrah's
777 Harrah's Boulevard, Atlantic City, NJ, 08401
www.harrahs.com

Sands
Indiana Avenue and Brighton Park, Atlantic City, NJ, 08401
www.sandsac.com

Tropicana
Brighton Avenue and The Boardwalk, Atlantic City, NJ, 08401
www.tropicana.net

Trump Taj Mahal
1000 Boardwalk at Virginia Avenue, Atlantic City, NJ, 08401
www.trumptaj.com

LAS VEGAS

Arizona Charlie's Decatur
740 S. Decatur Blvd, Las Vegas, NV, 89107
www.arizonacharlies.com

Bally's
3645 Las Vegas Blvd South, Las Vegas, Nevada, 89109-4307
www.caesars.com/ballys/lasvegas

◆ ♣ ♥ ♠

Bellagio
3600 S. Las Vegas Blvd, Las Vegas, NV,
89109
www.bellagio.com

Binion's
128 Fremont Street, Las Vegas, NV,
89101

www.binions.com

Boulder Station
4111 Boulder Highway, Las Vegas, NV,
89121
www.boulderstation.com

Cannery
2121 East Craig Road, North Las Vegas,
NV, 89030
www.cannerycasinos.com

Circus Circus
2880 Las Vegas Blvd South, Las Vegas,
NV, 89109-1120
www.circuscircus.com

Excalibur
3850 Las Vegas Blvd South, Las Vegas,
NV, 89109
www.excalibur.com

Fiesta Henderson
777 W Lake Mead Drive, Henderson,
NV, 89015
http://henderson.fiestacasino.com

Fiesta Rancho
2400 North Rancho Drive, Las Vegas,
NV, 89130
http://rancho.fiestacasino.com

Flamingo
3555 Las Vegas Blvd South, Las Vegas,
NV, 89109-8919
www.flamingolasvegas.com

Gold Coast
4000 W. Flamingo Rd., Las Vegas, NV,
89103
www.goldcoastcasino.com

Golden Nugget
129 East Fremont St, Las Vegas, NV,
89101
www.goldennugget.com

Green Valley Ranch
2300 Paseo Verde Parkway, Henderson,
NV, 89052
www.greenvalleyranchresort.com

Harrah's
3475 Las Vegas Blvd South, Las Vegas,
NV, 89109
www.harrahs.com

Imperial Palace
3535 Las Vegas Boulevard South,
Las Vegas, NV, 89109
www.imperialpalace.com

♦ ♣ ♥ ♠

Jackie Gaughan's Plaza
1 Main St, Las Vegas, NV, 89101-6370
www.plazahotelcasino.com

Luxor
3900 Las Vegas Blvd South, Las Vegas,
NV, 89119
www.luxor.com

Mandalay Bay
3950 Las Vegas Blvd South, Las Vegas,
NV, 89119
www.mandalaybay.com

MGM Grand
3799 Las Vegas Boulevard South,
Las Vegas, NV, 89109
www.mgmgrand.com

Mirage
3400 Las Vegas Blvd South, Las Vegas,
NV, 89109
www.mirage.com

Monte Carlo
3770 S. Las Vegas Blvd, Las Vegas, NV,
89109
www.montecarlo.com

Palace Station
2411 West Sahara Avenue, Las Vegas,
NV, 89102
www.palacestation.com

Palms
4321 West Flamingo Road, Las Vegas,
NV, 89103
www.palms.com

Rio
3700 West Flamingo Road, Las Vegas,
NV, 89103
www.harrahs.com

Sahara
2535 Las Vegas Blvd South, Las Vegas,
NV, 89109
www.saharavegas.com

Sam's Town
5111 Boulder Highway, Las Vegas, NV,
89122
www.samstownlv.com

Silverton
3333 Blue Diamond Road, Las Vegas,
NV, 89139,
www.silvertoncasino.com

Stardust
3000 Las Vegas Blvd South, Las Vegas,
NV, 89109
www.stardustlv.com

Stratosphere
2000 Las Vegas Blvd South, Las Vegas,
NV, 89104
www.stratospherehotel.com

Sunset Station
1301 West Sunset Road, Henderson,
NV, 89014-6607
www.sunsetstation.com

Texas Station
2101 Texas Star Lane, Las Vegas, NV,
89030
www.texasstation.com

The Orleans
4500 West Tropicana Ave, Las Vegas,
NV, 89103
www.orleanscasino.com

Tropicana
3801 Las Vegas Blvd South, Las Vegas,
NV, 89109
www.tropicanalv.com

LOS ANGELES

Bicycle Casino
7301 Eastern Avenue, Bell Gardens,
California, 90201

Commerce Casino
6131 East Telegraph Road, Commerce,
California, 90040-2501

Crystal Park
123 East Artesia Blvd, Compton, CA,
90220
www.crytsalparkcasino.com

Hollywood Park
3883 W. Century Blvd, Inglewood, CA,
90303

Hustler Casino
1000 W. Redondo Beach Blvd, Gardena,
California, 90247

Normandie
1045 West Rosecrans Ave, Gardena,
CA, 90247-2601
www.normandiecasino.com

RENO

Atlantis
3800 South Virginia S, Reno, NV,
89502
www.atlantiscasino.com

Circus Circus
500 North Sierra Street, Reno, NV,
89503
www.circusreno.com

Club Cal Neva
38 East Second Street, Reno, NV,
89501-1410
www.clubcalneva.com

Eldorado
345 North Virginia Street, Reno, NV,
89501
www.eldoradoreno.com

Peppermill
2707 South Virginia Street, Reno, NV,
89502
www.peppermillreno.com

Reno Hilton
2500 East Second Street, Reno, NV,
89595
www.caesars.com/Hilton/Reno

♦ ♣ ♥ ♠

CANADA

CALGARY

Cash Casino
4040 Blackfoot Trail, Southeast
Calgary, Alberta, T2G 4E6
www.cashcasino.ca

Elbow River Inn & Casino
1919 Macleod Trail, Calgary, Alberta,
T2G 4S1
www.elbowrivercasino.com

EDMONTON

Baccarat Casino
10128-104 Avenue Northwest,
Edmonton, Alberta, T5J 4Y8

Casino Edmonton
7055 Argyll Rd, Edmonton, Alberta,
T6C 4A5

Casino Yellowhead
12464-153 St, Edmonton, Alberta,
T5V 1S5
www.casinoabs.com

Palace Casino
West Edmonton Mall, 2710,
8882-170 St, Edmonton,
Alberta, T5T 4J2
www.palacecasino.com

QUEBEC

Casino de Charlevoix
183 Rue Richelieu, La Malbaie, Quebec,
G5A 1X8
www.casino-de-charlevoix.com

VANCOUVER

Gateway Casino
611 Main Street, Vancouver, British
Columbia, V6A 2V5
www.gatewaycasinos.com/vancouver

Great Canadian Casino
Holiday Inn, 709 West Broadway,
Vancouver, British Columbia, V5Z 1J5
*www.greatcanadiancasino.com/
holidayinn*

WINNIPEG

Club Regent Casino
1425 Regent Avenue West, Winnipeg,
Manitoba R2C 3B2
www.casinosofwinnipeg.com

CARRIBBEAN

ANTIGUA

King's Casino
King's Building, King's Building
Heritage Quay, Saint John's, Antigua
www.kingscasino.com

ARUBA

Alhambra Casino
J. E. Irausquin Blvd 47, Oranjestad

Excelsior Casino
Holiday Inn SunSpree Aruba Resort,
J. E. Irausquin Boulevard 230, Palm
Beach, Aruba
www.excelsiorcasino.com

Stellaris Casino
Aruba Marriott Resort, L. G. Smith Blvd
101, Palm Beach

CURAÇAO
Breezes
8 Dr Martin Luther King Blvd,
Willemstad
www.breezescuracao.com

Hill Rose Casino
Trupial Inn Hotel, Groot Davelaarweg
5, Selina
www.trupialinn.com

Hilton Curaçao Resort
John F Kennedy Blvd, Piscadera Bay
www.hiltoncaribbean.com

San Marco
Columbustraat 7, Willemstad
www.sanmarcocuracao.com

DOMINICAN REPUBLIC
Casino Playa Chiquita
Avenida Martinez, Sosua

El Napolitano Hotel & Casino
Avenida George Washington 101
Santo Domingo

**The American Casino at Jack Tar
Village**
Playa Dorada, Puerto Plata
www.amcasgroup.com/puerto_plata

MARTINIQUE
Casino Batelière Plazza
Rue des Alizés, Schoelcher, 97233

SINT MAARTEN
Coliseum Casino
Frontstreet 74, Philipsburg, Sint
Maarten

Diamond Casino
Frontstreet 1, Philipsburg
www.diamondcasinosxm.com

Paradise Plaza Casino
Welfare Road 69, Cole Bay
www.atlantisworld.com/html/paradise

EUROPE
UK
LONDON
Clermont Club
44 Berkeley Square, London, W1X 5DB

Colony Club
24 Hertford Street, London, W1J 7SA
*www.crockfordslondoncasino.co.uk/
colony-casino*

Crockfords Club
30 Curzon Street, London, W1J 7SA
*www.crockfordslondoncasino.co.uk/
crockfords-casino*

♦ ♣ ♥ ♠

Stakis Regency Club
The Imperial Hotel, 61-66 Russell
Square, London WC1B 5JS

The Gutshot Club
44-48 Clerkenwell Road, London,
EC1M 5PS

The Grosvenor Victoria Casino
150-162 Edgware Road, London
W2 2DT
www.grosevenor-casinos.co.uk

EAST
Great Yarmouth Grosvenor Casino
Marine Parade, Gt Yarmouth, NR30 3JG
www.grosvenor-casinos.co.uk

Luton Grosvenor Casino
Dunstable House, 50 Dunstable Road,
Luton, LU1 1EE
www.grosvenor-casinos.co.uk

MIDLANDS
Broadway Casino
1-4 Broadway Plaza, 220 Ladywood
Middleway, Birmingham, B16 8LP

China Palace Casino
16 Hurst Street, Birmingham, B5 4BN
www.stanleycasinos.com

Coventry Stanley Casino
Fletchampsted Highway, Tile Hill Lane,
Coventry, Warwickshire, C4 9DW
www.stanleycasinos.com

Derby Stanley Casino
2 Colyear Street, Derby DE1 1LA
www.stanleycasinos.com

Nottingham Gala Casino
4 Maid Marian Way, Nottingham,
NG1 6HS
www.galacasinos.co.uk

Victoria Club
16-18 Victoria Street, Nottingham
www.thevictoriaclub.co.uk

Walsall Grosvenor Casino
Bentley Mill Way, Bentley, Walsall,
WS2 OLE
www-grosevnor-casinos.co.uk

Walsall Stanley Casino
8-9 Stafford Street, Walsall , WS2
www.stanleycasinos.com

NORTH WEST
The Castle Casino
64 Queens Promenade, Blackpool,
FY2 9QG

Blackpool Grosvenor Casino
Grand Hall Buildings, 15 Station Road,
Blackpool FY2 9QG
www.grosvenor-casinos.co.uk

**Empire Street Grosvenor Casino
(Manchester)**
2 Empire Street, Cheetham Hill,
Manchester, M3 1JA
www.grosvenor-casinos.co.uk

♦ ♣ ♥ ♠

Liverpool Grosvenor Casino
76-78 West Derby Road, Liverpool
L6 9BY
www.grosvenor-casinos.co.uk

Stanley Circus Casino
110 Portland Street, Manchester,
M1 4RL
www.stanleycasinos.com

Stanley Strand Casino
40–44 Princess Street, Manchester,
M1 6DE
www.stanleycasinos.com

Stanley Grand
1-3 Temple Court, Liverpool, L2 6PY
www.stanleycasinos.com

Stoke Stanley Casino
14-16 Broad Street, Hanley,
Stoke-On-Trent, FT1 4EU
www.stanleycasinos.com

NORTH-EAST

Bonaparte's Casino Club
17 Livesey Street, Sheffield, S2 2BL

Moortown Grosvenor Casino
Moortown Corner House,
343 Harrogate Road, Leeds, S17 6LD
www.grosvenor-casinos.co.uk

Napoleon's Casino Club
37 Bolton Road, Bradford,
West Yorkshire, BD1 4DR

Newcastle Grosvenor Casino
100 St James Boulevard, Newcastle-
upon-Tyne, NE1 4BN
www.grosvenor-casinos.co.uk

Sheffield Grosvenor Casino
Queens Road, Sheffield, S2 4DF
www.grosvenor-casinos.co.uk

Stockport Gala Casino
59 Wellington Street, Stockport
SK1 3AD
www.galacasinos.co.uk

SOUTH

Bournemouth Gala Casino
48 Westover Road, Bournemouth,
BH1 2BZ
www.galacasinos.co.uk

Brighton Grosvenor Casino
88/92 Queen's Road, Brighton ,
BN1 3XE
www.grosvenor-casinos.co.uk

Ramsgate Grosvenor Casino
The Pavilion, Harbour Parade,
Ramsgate, Kent, CT11 8LS
www.grosvenor-casinos.co.uk

Reading Grosvenor Casino
Queen's Road, Reading, RG1 4SY
www.grosvenor-casinos.co.uk

♦ ♣ ♥ ♠

Southampton Grosvenor Casino
Leisure World, West Quay Rd,
Southampton, SO15
www.grosvenor-casinos.co.uk

Southsea Grosvenor Casino
South Parade, Southsea, Hampshire
PO4 0SR
www.grosvenor-casinos.co.uk

Stanley Annabelle Casino
1-2 Portswall Lane, Bristol, BS1 1NB
www.stanleycasinos.com

Torquay Casino Club
Abbey Road, Torquay TQ2 5NR
www.stanleycasinos.com

WALES
Les Croupiers Casino Club
32 St. Mary's Street, Cardiff, CF1 2AB

SCOTLAND
Dundee Gala Casino
Earl Grey Place, Dundee, Scotland,
DD1 4DE
www.galacasinos.co.uk

Gala Riverboat Casino
61 Broomielaw, Glasgow, G1 4RJ,
www.galacasinos.co.uk

Stanley Berkeley Casino
2 Rutland Place, Edinburgh, EH2 2AD
www.stanleycasinos.com

Stanley Edinburgh Casino
5b York Place, Edinburgh, Scotland,
EH1 3EB
www.stanleycasinos.com

IRELAND
DUBLIN
Merrion Casino Club
97 Merrion Square, Dublin 2
www.merrioncasinoclub.com

Silks Club
24 Earslfort Terrace, Dublin 2

The Fitzwilliam Card Club
Clifton Hall, Lower Fitzwilliam St,
Dublin 2
www.fitzwilliamcardclub.com

CORK
Macau Sporting Club
16 St Patricks Quay, Cork

www.corkmacau@celtweb.com

AUSTRIA
BREGENZ
Casino Bergenz
Symphonikerplatz 3, Bregenz, 6900
www.bregenz.casinos.at

GRAZ
Casino Graz
Landhausgasse 10 Graz, 8010
www.graz.casinos.at

♦ ♣ ♥ ♠

INNSBRUCK
Casino Innsbruck
Hotel Hilton, Innsbruck, 6020
www.innsbruck.casinos.at

LINZ
Casino Linz
Rainerstrasse 2-4, Linz, 4020
www.linz.casinos.at

Concord Card Casino
Rudolfstrasse 4+6, Linz, 4040
www.ccc.co.at

VIENNA
Concord Card Casino
Geiselbergstrasse 9, Vienna, 1110

www.ccc.co.at

CZECH REPUBLIC
PRAGUE
Casino Bohemia
Prague Congress Centre, Prague, 140 00

Casino de Prague Le Hilton
Pobrezni 1, Prague, 186 00

Casino Palais Savarin
Na Prikope 10, Prague, 110 00
www.czechcasinos.cz

ESTONIA
TALLINN
Astoria Palace Casino
5 Vabaduse Square, Tallinn, 10146
www.montecarlo.ee

Bally's Casino
Köleri 2, Tallinn, 10150
www.ballys.ee

Casino London – Metropol Hotel
Mere pst. 8b, Tallinn, 10111
www.casinolondon.ee/english

Casino Sfinks
Pärnu mnt 21, Tallinn, 10141

FINLAND
HELSINKI
Grand Casino
Mikonkatu 19, Helsinki, 00100
www.grandcasinohelsinki.fi

FRANCE
PARIS
Aviation Club de France
104 Avenue des Champs-Elysées, Paris, 75008
www.aviationclubdefrance.com

Cercle Haussmann
22 Rue de la Michodière, Paris, 75002

Cercle Wagram
47 Avenue de Wagram, Paris, 75017

GERMANY

BERLIN

Spielbank Berlin
Marlene-Dietrich-Platz 1, Berlin, 10785
www.spielbank-berlin.de

DORTMUND

Casino Hohensyburg
Hohensyburgstrasse 200, Dortmund,
44265
www.westspiel.de

HAMBURG

Casino Reeperbahn
Reeperbahn 94-96, Hamburg, 20359
www.spielbank-hamburg.de

Spielbank Hamburg
Fontenay 10, Hamburg, 20354
www.spielbank-hamburg.de

LATVIA

RIGA

Casino Furors
Blaumana, 9, Riga, LV-1011

Casino Play & Boy
Brivibas, 96, Riga, LV-1001

LITHUANIA

VILNIUS

Aladdin Casino
21/2 Gedimino Avenue, Vilnius, 2000
www.olympic-casino.net

Casino Planet
Basanaviciaus 4, Vilnius, 2000
www.casinoplanet.lt

Tropicana – Reval Hotel Lietuva
www.olympic-casino.net

NETHERLANDS

AMSTERDAM

Holland Casino
Max Euweplein 62, Amsterdam, 1017
MB
www.hollandcasino.nl

UTRECHT

Holland Casino
Overste den Oudenlaan 2, Utrecht,
3527 KW
www.hollandcasino.nl

POLAND

WARSAW

Grand Hotel & Casino
ul. Krucza 28, Warsaw, 00-522
www.orbis.pl

Marriott Hotel & Casino
23 Belwederska St, Warsaw, 00-697
www.casinospl.com.pl

Sofitel Victoria Hotel & Casino
ul. Krowleska 11, Warsaw, 00-065
www.orbis.pl

♦ ♣ ♥ ♠

ROMANIA

BUCHAREST

Casino Fortuna
World Trade Centre Street, Anastasia
Panu 26, Bucharest
www.casinofortuna.ro

Casino Partouche – Athenee Palace Hilton
Strada Episcopiei 13, Bucharest,
0217000

Grand Casino
Calea 1 3 Septembrie nr. 90, Bucharest,
0217000

Lido Casino
C.A. Rosetti Street, 13, Bucharest,
1617000

Marriott Grand Hotel & Casino
Calea 13 Septembrie, 90, Bucharest,
1227000
www.marriott.com

Plaza Casino Club
Calea Victoriei 163, Bucharest,
0217000

RUSSIA

MOSCOW

Carnaval City
Zelyony Prospect, 81, Moscow, 111558

Casino Admiral
Izmaylovskoye Shosse, 171, Hotel
Izmaylovo, Moscow

Casino Alexander Block
12A Krasnopresnenskaya
Naberezhnaya, Moscow, 123610
www.nakorable.ru

Casino Baccarat
Vavilova, 69, Moscow, 117997

Casino Baltiya
Novorizhskoye Shosse, 8th km,
Moscow

Casino Beverly Hills
Kudrynskaya Square, 1, Moscow,
123242

Casino Cosmos
150 Prospect Mira, Moscow, 129366
www.hotelcosmos.ru

Casino Desperado
Baryshikha Street, 14, Moscow, 123627

Casino Imperia
Ulitsa Pravdy, 1, Moscow, 125040
www.casinoimperia.ru

Casino Kapitel
Pervaya Ostankinskaya Ulitsa, 53,
Moscow

Casino Manhattan
Yasnogorskaya Ulitsa, 2, Moscow

Casino Megapolis
Mitinskaya, 39, Moscow

♦ ♣ ♥ ♠

Casino Metropol – Metropol Hotel
Teatralny Proyezd, Moscow, 103012

Casino Udarnik
Ulitsa Serafimovicha, 2, Moscow,
119072
www.superslots.ru

Korona
Novy Arbat, 15, Moscow, 119019

Metelitsa Entertainment Complex
21 Novy Arbat, Moscow, 119019
www.metelitsa.ru

Shangri-la Casino
2 Pushkinskaya Square, Moscow,
127006
www.shangrila.ru

ST PETERSBURG
Casino Conti
Kondratyevskiy Prospect, 44,
St Petersburg, 195197
www.contigroup.ru

Casino Goodwin
Prospect Nauki, 25, St Petersburg,
195256
www.setcrp.ru/casino/goodwin

Casino Lux
Prospect Slavy, 21, St Petersburg,
192239

Casino Olympia
Liteiny Prospect, 14, St Petersburg,
191028
www.contigroup.ru

Casino Plaza
Naberezhnaya Makarova, 2,
St Petersburg, 199034

Taleon Club and Casino
Naberezhnaya Reki Moyki, 59,
St Petersburg, 191186

Vegas Casino and Sports Bar
6 Manezhnaya Square, St. Petersburg,
191011

SLOVAKIA
BRATISLAVA
Park Casino
Hviezdoslavovo námestie 21,
Bratislava, 811 02
www.bratislavahotels.com

Regency Casino
Hodzovo námestie 2, Bratislava, 81625

SLOVENIA
LJUBLJANA
Casino Ljubljana
Astral Hotel, Ljubljana, 1000
www.astralhotel.com

♦ ♣ ♥ ♠

SPAIN

BARCELONA

Casino de Barcelona
C/Marina, 19-21, Barcelona, 08005
www.casino-barcelona.com

LANZAROTE

Casino de Lanzarote
Avenida de las Playas, 12, Lanzarote, 35510
www.casinodelanzarote.com

MALLORCA

Casino de Mallorca
Ubanización Sol de Mallorca, Calvia, Mallorca, 07181
www.casinodemallorca.com

SWEDEN

GOTHENBURG

Casino Cosmopol Gothenburg
Packhusplaten 7, Gothenburg
www.casinocosmopol.se

MALMÖ

Casino Cosmopol Malmö
Kungsparken, Malmö, 211 33
www.casinocosmopol.se

STOCKHOLM

Casino Cosmopol Stockholm
Kungsgatan 65, Stockholm
www.casinocosmopol.se

SWITZERLAND

MONTREUX

Casino Barrière de Montreux
Rue du Théâtre 9, Montreux, 1820

AFRICA

SOUTH AFRICA

DURBAN

Suncoast Casino and Entertainment World
1 Battery Beach Road, Durban, 4359
www.suncoastcasino.co.za

JOHANNESBURG

Caesar's Gauteng Hotel Casino
64 Jones Road, Johannesburg, 1620
www.caesars.co.za

NEWCASTLE

Monte Vista Hollywood Casino
112 Drakensberg Road, Newcastle, 2940

OCEANIA

AUSTRALIA

CANBERRA

Casino Canberra
21 Binara Street, Canberra, Australian Capital Territory 2601
www.casinocanberra.com.au

♦ ♣ ♥ ♠

MELBOURNE

Crown Casino
8 Whiteman Street, Southbank 3006,
Melbourne
www.crowncasino.com.au

WESTERN AUSTRALIA

Burswood International Resort Hotel & Casino Hotel
Great Eastern Highway, Burswood,
Western Australia 6100

NEW ZEALAND

CHRISTCHURCH

Christchurch Casino
30 Victoria Street, Christchurch, 8001
www.chchcasino.co.nz

DUNEDIN

Dunedin Casino
118 High Street Dunedin, 9001
www.dunedin.casino.co.nz

Useful poker websites

www.cardplayer.com
Includes reports, articles, WSOP and WPT updates, odds calculators

www.gambling-poker.com
Presents the rules of poker including poker rules for over 35 games, poker tournament info, where to play, and more.

www.homepoker.com
Information resource for home poker games, including articles, free information, poker products and strategy.

www.playwinningpoker.com
Advice on poker strategy and how to play winning poker.

www.pokerineurope.com
Message board and coverage of European clubs and tournaments.

www.poker-in-the-uk.com
A definitive guide to poker throughout the UK and Ireland.

www.pokerlistings.com
Online poker guide, featuring large poker site directory, objective reviews on 71 online poker rooms etc.

www.pokerpages.com

Website devoted to poker, including an international directory of poker rooms, WSOP, WPT, tournament schedules, tips and strategies and so on.

www.pokersearch.com

Worldwide casino poker room directory of over 700 card rooms with tournament schedules, game listings, users' polls, trip reports and more.

www.pokersyte.com

Poker rules, poker strategies and strategy tips for Texas Hold'em, Omaha, seven-card stud and five-card stud poker games.

www.pokertips.org

Online poker strategy, poker rules, poker tips and reviews.

www.pokertop10.com

Features info from the best poker rooms online, to poker rules and best hands.

www.texasholdem-poker.com

Free Texas Hold'em poker resource page, providing poker strategies and tips to get your game in shape.

www.thepokerforum.com

Information on Texas Hold'em, tournaments , online poker, poker theory and strategy.

www.unitedpokerforum.com

United Poker Forum allows you to post your questions and answers about poker strategy, gambling and betting tips.

www.worldpokertour.com

Official site from sponsoring organization with overview, polls, and player profiles.

www.worldseriesofpoker.com

Official website for the World Series of Poker. Summary of events, tournament schedules, news and history.

♦ ♣ ♥ ♠

The WSOP Poker Hall of Fame

Binion's Horseshoe Casino in Las Vegas decided to inaugurate a Poker Hall of Fame in the late 1970s. The selection of inductees is, to say the least, esoteric, but it remains an interesting list.

The criteria for inclusion are:

- the gambler must have played poker against other top competition

- the gambler must have played in high-stakes games

- the player must have played consistently and well, and to be respected by their peers

- the player must have stood the test of time

The following register of Poker Hall of Famers is organized by date of induction:

1979

Johnny Moss
Patriarch of the game, and winner of the World No-Limit Texas Hold'em Championship in 1970, 1971 and 1974, among many other records. He died in 1997 aged 90. See pages 186–187.

Nick (Nik) 'the Greek' Dandolos
One of the original high rollers, he could lose millions of dollars (apparently) quite effortlessly. See pages 187–189.

Felton 'Corky' McQorquodale
Corky was an old time No-Limit rounder, remembered for introducing Texas Hold'em to Las Vegas in 1963.

Red Winn
A great all-rounder rounder. And a player with the right name. Eat your hearts out onliners.

Sid Wyman
One of the first ultra-professionals to dominate Vegas, away from the tables he was co-owner at various times of The Sands, The Riviera and The Dunes. Play was suspended at The Dunes for two minutes to mark his funeral in 1978.

James Butler 'Wild Bill' Hickok
The firtst of two honorary positions, the original larger-than-life cardsharp, and possibly the only player to have the hand named after him when he was dying rather than when he was winning. Lived fast, died young. See pages 32-33.

Edmond Hoyle (c.1672– 1769)
The grand old man of gaming, his honorary position in the Hall of Fame is due to his determination to record in print how games were, and should be, played. Hence *Hoyle's Games*, the Bible of all gamesters.

1980
T. 'Blondie' Forbes
The original travellin' man, a rounder who probably played in more towns than any other player.

1981
Bill Boyd
One of the finest Five-Card Stud players of all time, Boyd was a frequent winner of the event at the WSOP.

1982
Tom Abdo
A supercool player. Having suffered a heart attack at the table he calmly asked another player to mind his chips and save his seat, intending to return. He died later that night. What an exit.

1983
Joe Bernstein
A dapper travelling gamester of the old school.

1984
Murph Harrold
Widely held among aficionados to be the finest Kansas City Lowball (Deuce-to-Seven Draw) player ever.

1985
Red Hodges
A Seven-Card Stud ace.

1986
Henry Green
Born in Alabama, a classic road gambler and noted all-rounder.

1987
Walter Clyde 'Puggy' Pearson
Became WSOP title holder in 1973, an aggressive Seven-Card Stud player and distributor of poker wisdom. See pages 192–193.

♦ ♣ ♥ ♠

1988
Doyle 'Texas Dolly' Brunson
For many the dominant senior poker player of modern years, winning the WSOP titles in 1976 and 1977, and the first player to win $1 million in tournament play. See pages 190–192.

Jack 'Treetops' Strauss
At 6 foot 6 inches, this towering Texan figure was WSOP title winner in 1982. See pages 193–194.

1989
Fred 'Sarge' Ferris
Born in New England of Lebanese parents, Ferris took up poker to escape poverty. The 1980 Kansas City Lowball (Deuce-to-Seven Draw) world champion, three years later, the IRS interrupted his game at the Horseshoe Casino to confiscate $46,000 in chips.

1990
Benny Binion
A great all-rounder, cool player, and one of the first player/entrepreneurs, founding the Horseshoe Casino in downtown Las Vegas, and inaugurating the WSOP in 1970. Selected for the Hall of Fame in 1986, he was enshrined the year after his death. See pages 40–42.

1991
David Edgar 'Chip' Reese
Aged only 40 when inaugurated, he was, at the time, the youngest Hall of Famer. Reese was born in Ohio and attended Dartmouth College, playing poker from his boyhood, initially for baseball cards . He hit Las Vegas in 1974 with a $400 stake, and simply rose to become one of the great professional all-rounders.

1992
Thomas Austin 'Amarillo Slim' Preston
One of poker's great ambassadors, he won the WSOP in 1972, and rapidly became a media star, gaining poker widespread respectability with his style and wit. Rarely seen at major tournaments in recent years, he nevertheless remains a household name. See pages 189–190.

◆ ♣ ♥ ♠

1993
'Gentleman Jack' Keller (b. 1943)
An astonishingly consistent and notably polite player. Philadelphia-born and Mississippi-based, Keller won the WSOP title in 1984, four short years after first arriving in Las Vegas.

1996
Julius Oral 'Little Man' Popwell
Another old-style player who had showdowns against the likes of Johnny Moss and Henry Green on the travelling circuit of the 1940s and '50s. He specialized in Five-Card Stud.

1997
Roger Moore
The son of a sharecropper, this consistent and determined player hasn't missed a WSOP tournament since 1974, and has been placed in the money 15 times, winning the WSOP $5000 Seven-Card Stud world title in 1994, and hitting the money spots a further three times.

2001
Stu Ungar
Another posthumous entry, it is odd that WSOP didn't inaugurate him earlier, as Ungar is widely regarded as the greatest poker player of all time, winning two WSOP titles before the age of 26, and ten No-limit Texas Hold'em championships. With Johnny Moss, the only person to have won the WSOP three times. See pages 200–203.

Now, when are WSOP going to inaugurate any women?

♦ ♣ ♥ ♠

World Series of Poker 2005–06 Season Fixtures

Grand Casino, Tunica	Aug. 11–25, 2005
Harrah's, Las Vegas	Sep. 6–16, 2005
Grand Casino, Biloxi	Cancelled
Caesars, Indiana	Oct. 19–Nov. 2, 2005
Paris/Bally's, Las Vegas	Nov. 9–22, 2005
Showboat, Atlantic City	Nov. 28–Dec. 9, 2005
Grand Casino, Tunica	Jan. 5–26, 2006
Harrah's, Atlantic City	Feb. 7–17, 2006
Caesars, Atlantic City	Mar. 21–31, 2006
Caesars, Palace Las Vegas	Apr. 3–14, 2006
Harrah's, New Orleans	May 18–28, 2006 *(Under Review)*
Harrah's, Lake Tahoe	Jun. 6–16, 2006
2006 Toc At Rio	Jun. 28–29, 2006
2006 Wsop At Rio	Summer 2006

Schedule subject to change.

♦ ♣ ♥ ♠

World Poker Tour – Season Four

The Mirage, Las Vegas	May 23–26, 2005
Aviation Club De France, Paris	Jul 25–29, 2005
The Bicycle Casino, Bell Gardens	Aug 27–31, 2005
Borgata, Atlantic City	Sep. 19–22, 2005
Ultimatebet, Aruba	Sep. 26–Oct. 3 2005
Bellagio, Las Vegas	Oct. 18–23, 2005
Foxwoods Resort Casino, Mashantucket	Nov. 13–16, 2005
Bellagio, Las Vegas	Dec. 13–16, 2005
PokerStars, Atlantis Resort, Bahamas	Jan. 4–11, 2006
Gold Strike, Tunica	Jan 22–26, 2006
Commerce, Commerce	Feb. 17–21, 2006
Commerce, Commerce	Feb. 22–23, 2006
Bay 101, San José	Feb. 27–Mar. 3, 2006
PartyPoker	Mar. 12–19, 2006
Reno Hilton, Reno	Mar. 27–30, 2006
Bellagio, Las Vegas	Apr. 18–24, 2006

♦ ♣ ♥ ♠

Index

Definitions of most important poker terms and slang can be found in alphabetical order in The Language of Poker chapter (pages 46-74) and thus, for reasons of brevity, and to avoid confusion, are not listed in the Index.

♦ ♣ ♥ ♠

♦ ♣ ♥ ♠